The Ultimate Peru Travel Guide 2024-2025

Things to Know before Travelling to Peru, Expert picks for your Vacation, Top Things to do, Budget and Safety Tips

HILDA CATHY

COPYRIGHT

CONTENTS

INTRODUCTION

The fabled atmosphere of the Inca Empire's homeland, Peru, has persisted to this day. Cuzco, the cultural hub of Peru, offers a window into the country's glorious past as the Sacred Valley's epicenter and the starting point for expeditions to the mythical lost city of Machu Picchu. A vibrant Peruvian art, architecture, and music scene has emerged because of the fusion of Quechua and Aymara traditions, which trace their ancestry back to the Incas and Spanish colonization. A tourist visiting Peru may see the Pacific sun setting, climb the snowiest mountain in the Andes, and maybe even see a pink river dolphin in the Andes.

Ancient History

Peru, as we know it now, is based on a legendary past. Housing for humans has been recorded since the sixth century B.C. By 1500 B.C., a number of distinctive Peruvian civilizations had emerged, each with more structured village patterns. The most well-known of these ancient cultures are the Chavin and the Sechin, who created intricate jaguar-themed sacred imagery in the form of stone sculptures. A new wave of unique civilizations emerged when these old ones faded away. The Saliner and the Paracas were known for their intricate weavings and kiln-fired pottery. The enigmatic Nazca civilization sprang out of the Paracas civilization.

The Nazca people were responsible for creating the remarkable Nazca lines. These lines are part of a larger geoglyphic art installation that spans more than fifty kilometers over the desert in southern Peru. The well-known monkey, spider, bird, and waving human figure are among these designs, along with a number of smaller lines and sketches. The designs are so massive that they can only be barely seen from vantage points far above. Where the enigma begins is in the fact that they are best interpreted from above. Since the Nazca inhabitants were unable to see their own designs from above, we must wonder what inspired the architects to create them. Especially enigmatic is the waving figure; for what purpose was it created? In order for tourists to draw their own conclusions, a Peruvian trip should include a visit to the Nazca Lines.

The great Inca civilization emerged in Peru at the same time that the Nazca and other contemporaneous civilizations started to crumble. Midway through the fifteenth century, in the Cuzco valley, a little "municipality" gave rise to the Incan civilization. Even as the Inca Empire expanded, Cuzco maintained its status as the political and military capital. The Incan Empire extended from what is now Colombia to what is now northwest Argentina in just a century. Cuzco, the Incan capital and once-wealthiest city in the Americas, was also the center of the empire. Travelers visiting Peru can still walk the contour of the jaguar-shaped structure.

Although the Incas' expansion was mostly due to their superior military might and strategic planning, it was also due to their ability to adopt the finest features of the civilizations they subjugated. It was usual practice to send agents to foreign kings, who would often agree and bring their children to Cuzco for education, facilitating peaceful absorption.

The conclusion of a disruptive civil war between two Incan emperors occurred in 1532, the same year that Francisco Pizarro arrived on the Pacific coastlines of the Ecuadorian area. He and his entourage swiftly conquered the empire's northern territory after assassinating Atahualpa (for more on this, see the page on Ecuador). After sacking Cuzco, Pizarro proceeded south. For a number of years, the Incas fought ferociously; among their final strongholds was the long-lost city of Machu Picchu. Already, the Spanish had established their control. Although the Incas vanished along with their cities due to the spread of smallpox and other European illnesses, the region's magnificent masonry and architecture remained. Machu Picchu emerges from the clouds as the sun rises, and the jaguar of Cuzco continues to raise its head.

Recent History

For the next many centuries, Spain maintained control of Peru as a colony. Royalist forces-maintained control of Peru even as independence movements shook the rest of South America. In 1821, it became the last nation to declare its independence.

Conflicts between the military and political factions caused the young nation to tremble. Between 1879 and 1883, Peru was a defeated participant in the War of the Pacific with Chile. Radical changes, political unrest, and military coups defined the country's subsequent decades. After a time of relative calm under Alberto Fujimori's administration, the country's leaders demanded his resignation in 2000 on charges of corruption and human rights abuses.

Current politics

Alejandro Toledo is the president of Peru at the moment. There are many political parties in Peru's multi-party presidential representative democratic republic. The president appoints everyone in the Council of Ministers, including the Prime Minister. The traditional Peruvian government is structured with an executive, legislative, and judiciary branch.

Disputes over Peru's borders with Chile and Ecuador have long defined the country's foreign policy. But it was one of the first countries to join the Andean Community. During 2006 and 2007, Peru served as an elected member of the United Nations Security Council.

A Dramatic Landscape

Peru is a huge nation with a wide variety of breathtaking natural scenery. Hot rainforests, sandy beaches, and towering mountains are all possible sights on a Peruvian vacation. The northern end of Peru's lengthy coast is home to some stunning beaches perfect for surfing and sunbathing, while the southern end is adorned with hills and cliffs. Parts of the southern shore disappear into the desert, which has breathtaking sand dunes. Located in southern Peru, close to the picturesque white city of Arequipa, the Colca Canyon is a must-see for daring tourists.

Perhaps the most famous part of Peru is its Andean highlands. This breathtaking mountain range runs the length of the nation. Both the Cordillera Occidental and the Cordillera Oriental run parallel to one another. On the Altiplano, you may find the Andes at their broadest, and at a dizzying 22,500 feet, you can find Huascaran at their highest point. Tourists visiting Peru who are interested in climbing mountains will find this a suitable destination. Much of Peru's population resides in the Andean foothills and basins.
The world's highest lake, Lake Titicaca, is nestled in the southern Andes basin, close to the Bolivian border. This area is also home to both active and dormant volcanoes.

Iquitos is home to the headwaters of the great Amazon River, which forms the eastern border of Peru. Salva alta refers to the northern section of the jungle, while Selva baja describes the southern sections, which are characterized by river terraces and undulating plains. Parts of the dense and remote Peruvian jungle are only accessible by river.

Environmental Issues

The Amazon rainforest in Peru is vital for several reasons, including the fact that it is home to indigenous peoples, a powerhouse for sequestering atmospheric carbon dioxide, and a habitat for many species that are otherwise nowhere else on Earth. This priceless area is in danger from logging, oil exploration, farming, chemical spraying against coca cultivation, mining, and other resource extraction activities that have been prioritized by previous leadership regimes in the nation. The Peruvian government has not yet taken a significant step to address the problem of unsustainable and harmful behaviors, while there are several independent groups that are actively working towards this goal.

Peru continues to have issues with the illicit sale of these delicate creatures, despite being a party to the Convention on the International Sale of Endangered Species. Ten species in Peru are considered critically endangered, twenty-eight species are endangered, and ninety-nine species are vulnerable, according to the Convention.

More information may be available from the Peruvian Association for the Conservation of Nature, AymaraNet, Quechua Network, and the Peruvian Amazon Indian Network, among other prominent Peruvian groups that are involved in these and other environmental concerns. Peruvian tourists may do their part by learning about the country's environmental issues and planning their trips accordingly.

A World of Wildlife

The coast, Andes, and Amazon River provide Peru with a very unique landscape, contributing to its unparalleled biodiversity.

The most breathtaking of the country's 53 protected areas is Manu. Even though getting there isn't exactly a picnic (you have to take a river or plane), it's well worth it to see the most ecologically varied region of the Peruvian Amazon. A staggering variety of butterflies, as well as thirteen species of primates, one thousand bird species, and twenty-two species of animals, call the reserve home.

The rainforest is home to a variety of wildlife, including howler, spider, wooly, sloth, and armadillo monkeys, among others. Along the Amazon, you may see both common and exotic creatures, including tapirs, peccaries (a pig-like animal), and river otters. Rainforest animals like jaguars, pumas, ocelots, caimans, and giant snakes are common; thus, tourists consider themselves fortunate if they don't encounter any of them. Seeing a pink river dolphin in the Amazon is also considered a fortunate charm for tourists.

Along with a kind of bear, the Andes are home to big cats. Alpacas and llamas, the national animals of Peru and known for their luxurious fleece, are sure to be seen on any trip to the country. In order to see the magnificent Andean condor, visitors to the Colca Canyon and the Andes need to keep their eyes peeled. Dolphins, sharks, and sperm whales are common sights along Peru's coastline.

Weather

As varied as Peru's terrain is, so too is its weather. From January through March, the nation has its rainiest season.

While the coast is pleasant and slightly humid at this time, sunbathers should be aware that the beaches are perpetually misted throughout the remainder of the year.
Even though there are usually spectacular cloudbursts in the afternoon, the highlands of Peru, including sites like Cuzco and Lake Titicaca, have cooler temperatures throughout
the rainy season. The lowest temperatures often occur between June and August; however, this is still the busiest tourist season. Keep in mind that some of these regions are rather high, and the evenings may be below freezing.

Because it is a rainforest, the Amazon is always muggy, although the rains lessen somewhat between May and October. The amount of rain that might disrupt a vacation is rather unusual, especially during the rainy season. The weather here is hot all year round; however, you may need to bundle up at night because of the temperature drops.

Peruvian Culture

Peruvian culture is a stunning fusion of indigenous and Hispanic elements. Native speakers of Peru's Quechua and Aymara languages make up the country's two largest indigenous populations. Despite the slow but steady advance of globalization, these proud Inca descendants have managed to maintain and even advance their civilizations. Indeed, many people still consider Cuzco, the ancient Inca capital, to be the cultural center of Peru.

The traditional clothing of Peru is stunning. Women in various locations wear polleras, which are layers of colorful skirts. Some of them wear cotton petticoats with intricate patterns beneath their black skirts, while others wear belts that are large and embroidered. In the highlands of Peru, where winters can be brutal, ponchos are an absolute must. Ponchos from Cuzco are shorter, while those from Cajamarca and Puno are lengthy and showy. Many people also wear hats made of straw or wool.

Seeing some of Peru's contemporary and historic art is a must on every Peruvian vacation. Jewelry, weavings, stone and metal sculptures, and other pre-Spanish artifacts are remarkable instances of creative expression. A multi-faceted artistic tradition has emerged out of the mestizo and indigenous painting traditions that emerged during colonial times. Arequipa, a

colonial city in Peru, is a prime example of the country's stunning architecture. The cobblestone lanes are adorned with white churches and
facades, while the twisting avenues are dotted with architectural marvels, ranging from historic palaces and cottages to monasteries.
Machu Picchu, the lost city of Peru, stands head and shoulders above all other ancient cities due to its exceptional engineering and strategic placement. The stone salons and temples protrude straight from the summit of the mountain, which precipitates down to the rivers below on all sides. The tiered gardens showcase the Incas' agricultural prowess, while the astrological marks attest to their extraordinary astronomical acumen. There are few things more awe-inspiring than the Lost City. A Peruvian tour is sure to include a variety of Peruvian musical styles, each with its own unique flavor. It combines the gentle stringed instruments of Spain with the wind and percussion influences of pre-Columbian America.

A World-Famous Cuisine

Peruvian food is gaining fame all around the globe. The traditional Peruvian staples of rice, potatoes, and maize—which have absorbed flavors from Basque, Spanish, and Asian cuisines—have given rise to a refined genre. Indulge in some gourmet treats while on a cruise to Peru.
Coastal restaurants provide delicious ceviche's and other seafood delicacies. Milk, Chile pepper, or potatoes are common Peruvian additions to these recipes. Various potato-based meals, often accompanied by soup, are popular in different regions, as are tamales and humitas. Almost all Peruvian dishes come with a hearty soup or stew.

Cuy, often known as roast guinea pig, is a dish that adventurous diners could enjoy. Guests at Andean restaurants often enjoy alpaca meat with yucca, a delicious root vegetable native to the region, and other highland specialties.

Fusion cuisine, traditional recipes in flux, and world cuisine at its finest are all created in Lima. Before continuing on their journey, tourists should dine at one of the city's numerous excellent restaurants.

Because of the wide range of activities available, the stunning and diverse Peruvian landscape has become one of the world's most popular tourist destinations. Stunning natural beauty, rich cultural heritage, ancient Inca sites, and delicious, internationally acclaimed cuisine are just a few of the many attractions.

1. Machu Picchu, one of the 7 Wonders of the World

This is an obvious choice. Machu Picchu will always be named as the number one item on the bucket list of anybody who has traveled to Peru. The "Lost City of the Incas" is a legendary site that is said to be unlike any other, thanks to its eerie atmosphere, rich history, and ruins, all of which were created as a regal retreat for the upper Inca aristocracy. Every year, millions of tourist's flocks to this once-Inca stronghold, making it the most popular tourist site in South America since its discovery.

2. The sunny beaches (La costa)

Countless breathtaking beaches dot Peru's expansive coastline, which extends more than 1,550 miles (2,500 km). Peru has everything you might want for a vacation: warm waters at one of the numerous resorts, surfing the world's largest wave, or a stroll along Lima's beachfront overlooking the ocean.

3. The highlands (La sierra)

The Andes make up about one-third of Peru's territory and are home to several mountain ranges, valleys, archaeological sites, and indigenous populations. It is a popular destination for hikers due to the unparalleled beauty of the region's amazing scenery. Cusco, Arequipa, and Huaraz are just a few of the famous highland cities that call the Andes Mountains home.

4. The amazon (La selva)

The Amazon Rainforest is the largest territory in the country, covering nearly 60% of it. The Peruvian rainforest is a haven for a vast array of plant and animal species, making it an ideal destination for ecotourists and animal enthusiasts. There are a lot of national parks and protected areas in the area; therefore, ecotourism has been on the rise, so you can see the animals without destroying them.

5. The mouthwatering food

If you ask me, the food and culture of Peru are incentive enough to go there. The three areas of Peru that were already mentioned—the coast, the highlands, and the jungle
contribute to the vast ingredient and recipe repertoire that is Peruvian cuisine. Every meal gets its own flavor from the many local and international mixes and fusions that originate from these places. We highly recommend the ceviche, lomo saltado, and aji de gallina, three of our favorite dishes.

6. Infinite amount of treks

Peru is a trekker's dream due to its varied terrain and several mountain ranges. The Salkantay Trek, the Inca Trail, and the Huayhuash Circuit are just a few of the popular treks that draw visitors from all over the globe. On every hike, you'll be greeted with breathtaking beauty that will stay with you forever. Additionally, some have opportunities to cycle, zipline, rock climb, and more, which enhances the experience.

7. The diverse and native wildlife

It may come as a surprise, but Peru is a megadiverse nation with some of the world's most incredible wildlife. Penguins, boobies, jaguars, and sloths are among the many species found here, in addition to the cute and cuddly alpacas and llamas. In addition, the Peruvian dog, the spectacled bear (the inspiration for Paddington Bear), the pink river dolphin, the puma, and the Andean condor are all uncommon indigenous species.

8. The rich art, culture, and history

From the north to the south and the east to the west, Peru is a land of many cultures. There are hundreds of indigenous groups spread out around the nation, and their traditions have blended with those of Europeans, Africans, and Asians. The customs and history of each of these have developed over time or evolved in response to the country's rapid modernization.

9. Ayahuasca retreats

Ayahuasca, a plant medicine, has recently gained popularity among both residents and visitors for its purported ability to aid with cancer and other medical issues, as well as with self-discovery, spiritual breakthroughs, and understanding the essence of life. The traditional usage of the psychedelic ayahuasca brews is still practiced today, with small groups of indigenous curanderos (healers/shamans) in forest or Andean settings. The "journey" and experience are unparalleled, and many have emerged from them with a fresh perspective on life.

10. Lake Titicaca, the highest navigable lake in the world

Said to be the "Birthplace of the Incas," Peru and Bolivia share the border with the breathtakingly high Lake Titicaca, which rises an incredible 1,2,500 feet (3,800 m) above sea level. It has more than forty islands, one of which is the intriguing artificial Floating Islands of Uros. As you float peacefully around Lake Titicaca on a boat, you may learn about the history and culture of the islands that make up the lake.

11. It's affordable

Peru is one of the most budget-friendly South American nations to visit. Many goods and services are available at low rates, and the exchange rate is beneficial compared to more established currencies. You may have a lavish vacation without breaking the bank if you plan it properly.

12. Pisco Sour, Peru's signature cocktail

This sweet and sour cocktail is very Peruvian, made with pisco, the national drink of Peru! Guests at Lima's Gran Hotel Bolivar have included Walt Disney, Ernest Hemingway, Orson Welles, and Nat King Cole, thanks to the distinctive taste of the fizzy pisco drink!

13. Huacachina, the only natural oasis in South America

The gorgeous, always bright Huacachina oasis is about five hours' drive from Lima. A haven for adventurers and beach bums alike, with some of the world's largest sand dunes. Soak up some rays by the pool, stroll the oasis, or, for the ultimate adrenaline rush, try sandboarding or dune bugging. Tourists visiting Peru now consider it an absolute must-see.

14. The Ballestas Islands

Located off the coast of Paracas in the Pacific, the Ballestas Islands are about three hours away from Lima. They are known as the Peruvian Galapagos. Thousands of bird species, including penguins, sea lions, and dolphins, call the islands home, making them a paradise for nature lovers. Going on a trip to the Ballestas is the best way to see these creatures in their native environment.

15. The mysterious Nazca Lines

Around seventy hand-drawn forms, creatures, and figures dot the desert floor of Nazca, with some lines ranging in length from fifty to one hundred and twenty feet! The fact that these geoglyphs are inaccessible to the naked eye makes them all the more mystifying, and most visitors discover this fact while on a guided tour flight. Even now, there is no consensus among historians and archaeologists on their creation, which has perplexed them for decades.

CHAPTER 1:

THINGS TO KNOW BEFORE YOU GO TO PERU

To Peru, the Andes Mountains are inseparable. This enormous mountain range, with its breathtaking scenery and numerous snow-capped summits, has an impact on all three of these aspects of the country's personality. It is important to note that Cusco serves as the entryway to the Inca Citadel of Machu Picchu if you are organizing a visit to this site. At an elevation of 3,399 meters above sea level, the air density in this city is much lower than that at sea level. This might lead to rapid fatigue and shortness of breath. Furthermore, Cusco is surrounded by mountains, one of which, Rainbow Mountain, may reach a height of 5,200 meters above sea level. What this means is that you should prepare yourself for a lot of slogs. If you're looking for a warm vacation spot in Peru, Cusco is a great option. The height and impact of this mountain should never be underestimated, however. Rest assured. Even a short stay at this high elevation might be disastrous for some people. Symptoms such as nausea, headaches, exhaustion, and difficulty breathing are possible. No one is safe from the effects of altitude sickness; however, some are more vulnerable than others. So, make sure this is the first thing you learn about Peru before you travel. The good news is that the coca leaves will be useful. For relief from altitude sickness and increased energy, try chewing some coca leaves or sipping some coca tea. In Cusco and the Andes, you may find coca leaves in plenty. Hotels, restaurants, and marketplaces are the most common places to see them. Generally speaking, you should relax and enjoy your first few days in Cusco. In particular, if you would prefer that your journey not present any difficulties. Hikes or exploring the sites in Cusco are best tackled when your body has adjusted to the higher elevation.

- **PLANNING IS KEY**

  Thousands of tourists visit Peru daily because of how popular it is. It is wise to plan ahead at all times. Machu Picchu sees hundreds of visitors every day, just to give you an idea. Consequently, there is a high level of interest. Preparing for your vacation will be somewhat stressful because of this. To get to the Inca Citadel, some hikers choose to use the Inca Trail. However, 500 visitors per day are allowed access to the Inca Trail by the Peruvian government. So, make sure the permissions are available if you're one of those daring people. It is advisable to buy your tickets and book your trips ahead of time because of this. Alternatively, you may consult with our consultants if you would rather not fret about the logistics of acquiring admission tickets or rail tickets. The ability to arrange for a guided tour is going to be quite helpful. The situation will be much more favorable if you have a well-planned schedule. Before you go, make sure you study the company. Only choose trustworthy service providers. Peruvian security is usually OK; however, it's better to be safe than sorry. If you want your vacation to Peru to be an unforgettable experience, making your reservations in advance is a must. Keep in mind that the Sanctuary of Machu Picchu has its own unique climate due to its location in a subtropical region. Knowing what to bring on a tropical trip is, therefore, a smart idea. One of the keys to an amazing vacation is knowing this.

- **COLD NIGHTS IN THE MOUNTAINS**

  Pay close attention to this item if you never spent any time in mountain ranges growing up in a flat location. One of the few things we often notice is altitude sickness. However, the temperature in Cusco can be too much for those who aren't used to frigid climates. It is downright chilly at night in Peru, particularly in Cusco. Get ready for a chilly night since the structures lack insulation and heating. Remember to pack warm clothing. The nights in the Andes may be bone-chillingly chilly, despite the balmy days. Know that the cold might strike at any moment. You should be prepared for the chilly weather if you want to take advantage of the various trips in Peru that go to the high Andean areas. If you want to take advantage of the Imperial City, it is wise to bring along some warm clothing. You should be concerned about packing watertight garments if your trip falls during the wet season. You won't discover both frosts and showers since they often occur in different seasons.

- **TAP WATER IS NOT SAFE TO DRINK**

  This is one of the most important things to keep in mind before your trip to Peru. Water contamination is a major issue in Peru. There is no way that our water is fit for human consumption. Nobody drinks the water from the faucet, not even us natives. Chlorine, being the primary means of removing contaminants and germs, is present in high concentrations. This is why, for the best results, we boil the water before using it to purify it. Drinking untreated water may make you ill and ruin your vacation plans, so be sure to drink only filtered or purified water. Verify that the bottle cap is securely fastened and undamaged. A water filter may remove silt and certain toxins, and water purification pills can disinfect the water as well. This is something to think about while planning a trip to Peru and trying to figure out what to bring.

- **CASH IS KING**

  You should be aware of the local currency in Peru before you go there. Cash is king in Peru, even though most places accept a variety of payment options. Carrying along a little amount of cash is usually a good idea. For little purchases or for any unexpected needs that may arise along the journey. Having a significant quantity on hand is not necessary. Be cautious not to become a victim of thieves, but remember that it is important to have some spare cash on hand. While a large number of businesses accept credit cards, many others exclusively take cash. This is particularly true among Peru's finest dining venues. For instance, in the heart of Cusco, you can only find souvenir shops and little eateries that take cash. Unfortunately, even though there are many ATMs, those in more rural locations may have trouble using them. So, bear this in mind and be cautious on your Andean hikes. Our recommendation is that you inform your bank in advance of any international trip plans you may have. By doing so, you can verify the costs of making international ATM withdrawals.

- **KNOW THE CLIMATE**

  The weather in Peru may change drastically from one place to another. On the other hand, April through October is often the dry season in the Peruvian climate. In addition, the rainy season takes up the majority of the year. Similarly, the weather might be different depending on where you are. You may enjoy both dry and wet seasons in the mountain areas. Humidity, heat, and rain are all features of the rainforest. While, depending on the location, you may be able to enjoy mild weather with minimal rain, humidity, and heat along the ocean. The rainy season is the perfect time to enjoy some of Peru's tourism attractions. Just like Machu Picchu, the rainiest time of year also happens to be the least popular with tourists. Traveling around this period might be a smart move if you want to avoid huge crowds.

- **DON'T BE AFRAID TO HAGGLE**

  Almost anything in Peru can be bargained for. Of course, this won't work when trying to negotiate a price, such as when going to a restaurant or a museum. On the other hand, it's completely OK at outdoor markets or other souvenir stores. Bargaining is a great game to play with the vendor, even if you're not from around here. Also, keep in mind that dealers and merchants will charge you a premium if you are a tourist or foreigner. Therefore, negotiating a lower price is quite normal and anticipated. It is usual practice to slash prices by half or more, so don't be deceived. Get it done! You won't find it inexpensive; it's more like a sport. Enjoy yourself and immerse yourself in this remarkable culture. One of the numerous entertaining activities in Peru is haggling.

- **THE LANGUAGE OF PERU**

  Keep in mind that you will be smack dab in the midst of a Spanish-speaking nation when you plan your trip to Peru. Peru is home to speakers of several languages, not only Spanish. Peru is home to a wide variety of languages, some of which are more widely spoken than others. These later languages are unique to certain Andean areas of Peru and are spoken by indigenous peoples there. However, the majority of the population should be able to communicate well in Spanish. Not knowing Spanish? No problem. Learning the language will be an adventure, although in major cities, English is sufficient. Regardless, do your best with Spanish. Acquiring some basic words or bringing a small dictionary might be beneficial. You can comprehend basic discussions with the aid of one of the many smartphone apps available today.

10 BEST THINGS TO DO IN PERU – 2024

Besides hiking to Machu Picchu along the Inca Trail, Peru offers a plethora of other spectacular attractions. One of the first things you absolutely must do in Peru is to see the amazing Inca ruins! The remainder of the nation should be explored thereafter. It contains some very remarkable websites that you have likely never heard of.

Peru has been a dream come true for us on several occasions. It would take a lifetime to explore all Peru has to offer, but we can help you narrow it down to the top attractions. We recommend not missing out on a few things if you have a few weeks to spare. Here are some of our favorite things to do in Peru to help you plan your vacation.

1. Machu Picchu

Among the many Peruvian attractions, Machu Picchu is perhaps the most popular. This amazing city's Inca ruins are among Peru's most well-known tourist destinations, and rightfully so. The next morning, we got up extra early to see the sunrise at Machu Picchu. When I was out walking in the dark and saw a llama, it caught me off guard. The old ruins really have llamas all over them. Not only is Machu Picchu a World Heritage Site according to UNESCO, but it is also considered one of the New Seven Wonders of the World.

Unbelievable as it may seem, the Lost City of the Incas is located in an alien universe. It is difficult to fathom how the Incan Empire constructed this metropolis perched on a mountainside with terraces that plunge into the valley below. In 1911, Hiram Bingham brought Machu Picchu, often known as the Lost City of the Incas, to the attention of the Western world.

2. Hike The Inca Trail

There are few hikes as well-known or iconic as the Inca Trail. Many people's lifelong goals include hiking the Inca Trail. Hikers from all over the globe go to Peru to experience this iconic trail, which has been around for a very long time. Although reaching the Inca Ruins on the traditional Machu Picchu journey takes only three days, it is quite an ordeal. We recommend a longer trip since you will be walking for approximately seven hours daily.

3. Hike Rainbow Mountain

The ascent and descent of Rainbow Mountain is among the top Peruvian hikes. At an elevation of more than 14,000 feet, the day-long hike winds along a dirt road that passes between towering green and shocking red granite peaks. Along the way, you'll see charming stone cottages and sparkling mountain streams, leading up to a breathtaking panorama of multicolored mountains.

4. Cusco

The stunning colonial town of Cusco serves as the starting point for hikes to Machu Picchu. Cusco is not just a city that deserves a visit; it is also a UNESCO World Heritage Site. Once your plane touches down, you'll need some time to adjust to the high altitude (3300 meters above sea level). Relax and sip on some hot chocolate.

The Plaza de Armas, home to the Santo Domingo Cathedral and the Iglesia de la Compañía de Jesus, is an absolute must-see. Christ the Redeemer is located in Cusco, and the Twelve Angled Stone is a must-see. A twelve-sided stone was a component of an Inca citadel.

5. Sacred Valley

Seeing the Sacred Valley is a wonderful substitute for trekking to Machu Picchu. In Ollantaytambo, you will get the opportunity to tour a remarkable Inca city. While the majestic Andes Mountains encircled us, we wandered around its agricultural terraces.

6. Huacachina

The Peruvian town of Huacachina sits atop the Oasis of America, a man-made lake in the midst of a desert. You really must include this breathtaking site on your itinerary while in Peru. Huge dunes surround the lake, and hotels, restaurants, and guesthouses line its shores. For a little relaxation, it's the perfect spot.

7. Dune Hiking

It never occurred to me that Peru had a desert until I went there. And that's without even considering the massive 188,700 square km desert. Among the most breathtaking deserts I have ever laid eyes on, I had an absolute pleasure whizzing down its slopes. Observing the sun set from atop a dune was the most enjoyable thing I've ever done.

8. Sandboarding

Since snowboarding is one of our favorite winter sports, we couldn't resist trying sandboarding when we visited the world's tallest sand dunes. We were not quite as skilled while snowboarding. Edge carving is more challenging at first, but exhilarating after we master it.

9. Dune Buggy Tour

Here is something exciting to do in Peru if you're looking for an adrenaline rush. The dune buggy excursion was terrifying; I felt we would lose control on the steep dunes. Our hearts were racing; it was the wildest trip we'd ever been on.

10. Pisco Wine Tour

Peru is known for its excellent wine, right? In order to see the surrounding vineyards, we hired a driver from Huacachina for the day. The proprietors are kind and inviting, and they provide free tastings of their wine. During your stay, don't miss the opportunity to sample Pisco, the native spirit! Peruvians love their Pisco Sours, and for good reason.

CHAPTER 2:

BEST PERU FESTIVALS NOT TO MISS IN 2024

Cultural opportunities abound in Peru, a nation rich in history and varied cultures. Festivals in Peru provide a fascinating window into the rich tapestry of cultures and ethnicities that make up Peruvian identity; these celebrations have their origins in the country's varied history. These activities highlight Peru's dedication to maintaining and honoring its cultural and historical heritage, ranging from the ancient ceremonies of Inti Raymi, which are based on the history of the Inca Empire, to the syncretic spirituality of Qoyllur Rit'i, where indigenous beliefs blend with Catholic influences.

The artistic skill and creative emotions that characterize Peruvian festivals are on full display in the vibrant displays, elaborate dance routines, and breathtaking performances. Tourists may mingle with locals, experience new cultures, and make experiences that will last a lifetime during these festivities, which go beyond just visual spectacle. Culinary pleasures and the stunning landscapes and historical places of Peru come together in a sensory feast during the festivals, whether you're reveling in the patriotic fervor of Fiestas Patrias or discovering the worldwide craft beer industry at the Festival de la Cerveza. Because Peruvian festivals take place all year round, tourists may tailor their trip to their liking, guaranteeing an unforgettable experience that will put them in the middle of the country's vibrant culture.
There are many festivals in Peru, but a few stand out due to their rich histories, spectacular parades, and the strong sense of community they inspire.

1. Inti Raymi: A Celebration of Light and Legacy

In the majestic Andes, where the Inca culture once flourished, Cusco plays home to the magnificent Inti Raymi, also known as the Festival of the Sun. One evidence of the Incas' profound relationship with the universe is their celebration of the winter solstice, which occurs on June 24 in the Southern Hemisphere. The day starts with a ritual march to Sacsayhuamán, the stronghold, from Qorikancha, the Sun Temple. Participants pay respect to the sun deity Inti by reenacting ancient rites while dressed in magnificent traditional clothes.

Along with the spiritual force of the procession come the rhythmic pulses of traditional instruments, dancing, and song. Everyone, from players to spectators, is whisked away to a bygone era when the Inca Empire was at the height of its might as the city transforms into a living museum. Not only is it a party, but it's also a cultural immersion into Peru's ancient past.

2. Carnaval de Cajamarca: A Riot of Colors and Joy

In the last days of the dry season before the rains arrive, Cajamarca comes alive with Carnaval de Cajamarca, a festival of vibrant colors and contagious enthusiasm. This colorful carnival blends indigenous and Spanish customs and is held in the months of February or March, just before Lent. Exuberant water battles, music, and parades light up Cajamarca's streets.

Water fights that start out at random during Carnaval de Cajamarca are known for being both lighthearted and communal. As a fun and healthy way to celebrate the impending harvest season and the washing away of sins, locals and tourists alike get into water battles. This carnival is a perfect illustration of the cultural melting pot that is Peru, thanks to the traditional dance troupes who perform it in elaborate costumes.

3. Fiestas Patrias: A Nation's Resounding Independence

The whole country is filled with patriotic enthusiasm during Fiestas Patrias, which takes place on July 28th and 29th, marking Peru's National Independence Day. Military parades, cultural events, and fireworks take place in Lima's historic Plaza de Armas, making it the epicentre of large-scale festivities. The celebrations bring Peruvians together in national pride as they spread throughout the country.

There is more to Fiestas Patrias than just the spectacular parades; it is a time for neighbors and relatives to gather. Peruvian cultural events, street fairs, and traditional cuisine festivals showcase the country's vast and fascinating history. Fiestas Patrias gives tourists a taste of Peruvian culture and history, from the hoisting of the national flag to the sampling of traditional Peruvian cuisine, all while honoring the country's continuous independence movement.

4. Virgen de la Candelaria: A Dance of Devotion and Tradition

Virgen de la Candelaria is one of Peru's biggest traditional celebrations, held in Puno, which is located on the edge of Lake Titicaca. This celebration, which takes place in February, is a riot of traditional dances, elaborate costumes, and throbbing music. The procession commemorating the Virgin of Candelaria, a sacred figure in Catholicism, is the main event of the festival.

Drums beat at a steady pace, colorful skirts whirl, and dancing troupes from all over the world bring life to the streets. The rich cultural variety of Peru is reflected in the stories told via each dance, which have been passed down through generations. Communities come together in devotion and joy at the Virgen de la Candelaria festival, which is more than simply a pretty sight.

5. Semana Santa: A Journey Through Spiritual Reflection

Throughout Peru, people observe Semana Santa, also known as Holy Week, as a time for deep contemplation and religious devotion. Somber processions, religious observances, and communal gatherings characterize the week before Easter. Cusco, Ayacucho, and Lima are some of the cities that host spectacular passion plays.

Processions showcasing religious artifacts, sculptures of saints, and scenes from the Bible turn the streets into live theaters. The solemn but hypnotic ambiance, with its pervasive incense aroma, compels everyone in attendance and observers alike to reflect on the very nature of religion. As communities gather to remember the most sacred week in the Christian calendar, Semana Santa in Peru offers a rare chance to see how religious devotion and cultural expression meet.

6. Qoyllur Rit'i: A Pilgrimage of Spirituality and Tradition

The Qoyllur Rit'i pilgrimage, which takes place in the Sinakara Valley close to Cusco, is a holy and esoteric gathering that combines Catholicism with indigenous Andean traditions. During the event, which takes place in May or June, worshippers from all over the world make the pilgrimage to pay homage to the Lord of Qoyllur Rit'i. The Andean people's spiritual beliefs and the Catholicism introduced by the Spanish conquerors have remained intertwined, as this pilgrimage attests.

Sacred apus (mountain spirits) are honored at these festivities with traditional dances, rituals, and sacrifices. As they make their way over the mountainous terrain, pilgrims in their brilliant clothes add a rich tapestry of cultural expression to the already vibrant Andean scenery. Ancient Peruvian traditions and colonial influences come together in a profound pilgrimage to Qoyllur Rit'i, offering a rare glimpse into the eclectic character of Peruvian spirituality.

7. Festival de la Cerveza: A Toast to Peruvian Brewing Heritage

The Festival de la Cerveza is a wonderful introduction to Peruvian beer for anyone with an appreciation for the better things in life. This annual festival honors the nation's brewing tradition via sampling, live music, and cultural activities, and it takes place in different places at different times. It's a chance to sample traditional, high-quality Peruvian beer in all its many forms and tastes.

Local brewers showcase their greatest products, allowing beer connoisseurs and casual consumers alike to experience the richness of Peruvian brewing. The Festival de la Cerveza showcases a variety of beers from Peru's burgeoning craft beer culture, from intense IPAs to hearty stouts. Indulge your senses and meet the dedicated people who are driving Peru's booming craft beer sector at this year's event.

8. Gran Corso Wong: A Spectacle of Elegance and Extravagance

Lima, Peru's lively city, is home to the Gran Corso Wong, a spectacular parade that is sure to wow onlookers. Exquisite floats, live music, and mesmerizing dance performances are the hallmarks of this July celebration. During the Gran Corso Wong, Lima's streets are turned into a runway for exquisite innovation and creative expression.

Dancers and performers who showcase the rich variety of Peruvian culture carry intricately decorated floats through the city. The Gran Corso Wong showcases a visual feast that exemplifies the ever-changing character of Peruvian arts, ranging from classic dances to contemporary renditions. Lima, a city renowned for its delicious food and ancient sites, becomes even more charming during this magnificent procession.

BEST SEASONS TO VISIT PERU: A MONTH-BY-MONTH GUIDE

April–November is Peru's dry season, whereas December–March is the rainy season. While coastal areas don't get wet all year, the summer months (December to March) may be rather hot. While visitors go to Machu Picchu all year round, the shoulder seasons of September and November provide a welcome respite from the crowds while still enjoying mild weather and little precipitation. March and February are less than ideal because of the more frequent rain and cloudy weather. You may visit the Amazon Jungle at any time of year, although it's more enjoyable during the dry season. August is the festival month in Cusco when traditional dancers and marching bands bring the streets to life in celebration of the Inca sun festival, Inti Raymi, which takes place every year on June 24. At any time of year, you may learn about our many high-end Peru vacations.

- **Peru In January and February**

  Low season in Peru. Visits to Machu Picchu and the highlands have become less appealing due to the excessive rains and gloomy skies seen during these warm summer months. During the Amazon Jungle's high-water season, boaters may reach tributaries at greater depths and have a better chance of seeing a variety of animals that inhabit the forest canopy. The rainforest metropolis of Iquitos has typical summertime highs of 27 °C (81 °F). In February, Lima has scorching sunlight and mild temperatures, averaging 23 °C (74 °F) during the day and 20 °C (68 °F) at night. In Lima, the Pasacalles Parade commemorates the city's beginnings as La Ciudad de Los Reyes (The City of the Kings), while Puno's Virgin de la Candelaria Festival showcases a vibrant array of dancers and street art that draws heavily from the Quechua and Aymara traditions of the region.

- **Peru in March and April**

  Throughout March, the highlands of Peru see a persistent rainy season. Despite this, the average daily temperature is still 66 °F (18 °C). Cusco and Machu Picchu see a weather shift in April, a shoulder month. Although there is still occasional rain in April, it is a far more pleasant month to visit Peru because of the abundance of vegetation and the lack of crowds. Hot and dry conditions persist around the coasts of Peru and Lima, with temperatures reaching 80 °F (27 °C). As the Peruvian jungle enters its rainy season, which is characterized by high water levels and heavy rains, Cusco hosts the Semana Santa (Holy Week) festivities. Annual dates are subject to change. There is a significant spike in hotel prices, but the festivities more than compensate.

- **Peru in May and June**

  The highlands of Peru are entering their dry season, while rain is still possible until about the middle of May. Nighttime temperatures in Cusco, the Sacred Valley, and Machu Picchu decrease in June as winter approaches, with an average temperature of 66 °F (19 °C). Temperatures may dip below freezing at night, so pack accordingly if camping is a part of your hiking itinerary. The Amazon Jungle is seeing less rain than in the last several months, but the water levels remain high. The time of year when Cusco City, Peru, throws its most major celebrations. Sixty days following Easter Sunday, the vibrant and traditional Catholic celebration of Corpus Christi is performed, and every year on June 24th, there is a reenactment of the historic Inca sun festival known as Inti Raymi.

- **Peru in July and August**

  The weather in Cusco and Machu Picchu is typically dry with daily highs of about 64°F (18°C), a bright blue sky, and chilly evenings. Humid days average 86°F (30°C) and warm nights 71°F (22°C) in the northern and central Amazon regions of Peru. Clear skies are most likely to be present at this time (63%), making it an ideal time for jungle excursions and animal viewing. It takes four hours from Cusco to the village of Paucartambo, where the Fiesta de la Virgen del Carmen is held. The indigenous people of the area honor the saint with a procession through town called Mamacha Carmen, and they do it in front of a magnificent audience of costumed dancers and revelers. As part of the same celebration, a statue of the Virgen del Carmen is paraded through the historic district of central Lima from a church in the Barrios Altos area.

- **Peru in September and October**

  A shift is occurring in the highlands' climate. Cloudy mornings give way to sunny afternoons and evenings in the Cusco Region, where Machu Picchu is located. The weather is largely dry, although there is an increase in cloud cover in late October. The weather in Cusco typically ranges from 50°F (10°C) at night to 64°F (18°C) during the day. Although temperatures are somewhat lower, the Puno Region and Lake Titicaca experience the same. There will be a little more cloud cover and precipitation in the Peruvian Amazon. Typical temperatures range from a humid 89°F (32°C) to a normal 73°F (23°C). During the shoulder season, when temperatures are mild and fewer tourists visit, it is said to be the ideal time to visit Peru. The annual Mistura Food Festival is held in Lima. Around the latter week of October is when it usually happens. What a fantastic opportunity to taste the world-famous cuisine of Peru!

- **Peru in November and December**

  As summer approaches, weather patterns throughout the nation begin to shift. From December forward, daytime temperatures rise, and rainfall increases somewhat. Average daytime temperatures in Cusco are 65°F (18°C), while nighttime lows drop to 43°F (6°C). On December 23 and 24, Cusco hosts the Santikuraray market, also known as "The Selling of the Saints," as part of its Christmas celebrations. The market is located in Plaza de Armas, Cusco. The Andean people are known for their exquisitely crafted nativity scenes and gifts. Lima and Cusco have the liveliest New Year celebrations in Peru. Run around the main square seven times while dressed in yellow for good luck.

Peru is more than its ruins; seeing more of the country will reveal its enchantment. The Peruvian cuisine has gained international renown for its mastery of flavorful fusions inspired by the rich cultural traditions of Peru's native and immigrant populations. The Peruvians have a gift for welcoming people and their warm, genuine hug is both calming and enticing.

Language: It's quite significant. Prior to traveling to a foreign country, especially one where your native language is not widely spoken, it is crucial to have at least a basic understanding of the language.

Away from the popular tourist areas, you won't come across many Peruvians who speak English. Having guides and staff members who are fluent in English is often a perk of staying in five-star hotels or on a pre-arranged trip. If you're planning on traveling alone (particularly on a tight budget) or if you just want to immerse yourself in the local culture, it's a good idea to brush up on the fundamentals before you go.

The high learning curve makes getting going seem impossible at first. You could be amazed at how much Spanish you learn while traveling if you can master the fundamentals—the areas that are essential for everyday life.

Greetings

The ability to confidently and correctly say "hello" is a great confidence booster, even if you're far from being able to carry on a full-blown Spanish discussion. You may attempt to welcome locals by saying buenos días, buenas tardes, or buenas noches, depending on the situation.

Introductions

Attending a Peruvian social event as a non-Spanish speaker might be somewhat challenging. Even if no one speaks English, you should be prepared to handle the most typical first inquiry and introduction. Getting down to brass tacks:

What's your name? — ¿Cómo te llamas? (or the more formal Cómo se llama?)
My name is... — Me llamo... (or you can use mi nombre es...)
Then the typical opening question from those who don't already know the answer:

Where are you from? — ¿De dónde eres?
I'm from... — Soy de...

When you are introduced to someone, it's standard practice to say mucho gusto (it's a pleasure to meet you).

Numbers

As essential as it gets is the concept of numbers. They are essential in many places, including stores, transportation, and more. If you want to avoid using your raised fingers as a substitute for counting in Spanish, learning the language will help you a lot.

Time and Dates

You can go on to dates and times once you're comfortable with numbers. Almost every Peruvian will question you, "¿Qué hora es?" (What time is it?) if you're wearing a wristwatch. Even if it's just to start a conversation, it's a little awkward to stare at your own watch.

Shopping Basics

It won't take you long to become an expert Peruvian negotiator if you know your way around Spanish numbers and the local currency. Important terms comprise:

How much is it? — ¿Cuánto es? (or how much does it cost — cuánto cuesta?)
That's too expensive (for me) — Es demasiado caro (para mí).
There's a change shortage in Peru, so it's a good idea to check if the salesperson has change for larger bills: ¿tiene cambio? (Do you have change?). If you just want to browse (salespeople can be overly attentive in Peru), say sólo estoy mirando (I'm just looking).

Restaurants and Bars

Eating out is a great way to practice your Spanish every day, but the fundamentals aren't hard to pick up. Possible requirements may consist of:

The menu, please — La carta, por favor
The bill, please — La cuenta, por favor
What do you recommend? — ¿Qué me recomiendas?
Do you have vegetarian dishes—¿Tienes platos vegetarianos?

A beer, please — Una cerveza, por favor

Directions

For the most part, becoming disoriented in a strange land is an exciting experience. However, you'll need the local vernacular when you sense the urge to resume your journey.

I'm lost — Estoy perdido/a

How can I get to... — ¿Cómo puedo llegar a...

Where is the bus station? — ¿Dónde está (la estación de autobuses)?

Is it far? — ¿Está lejos?

Transportation Basics

Independent travelers frequently rely on Peru's numerous public transportation options, particularly those who travel with backpacks. Asking yourself some important questions before you leave and while you're on the road can make getting from point A to point B a much more pleasant experience. Here are some important points:

What time does the plane arrive? — ¿A qué hora llega (el avión)?

What time does the bus leave? — ¿A qué hora sale (el autobus)?

I want a ticket to ... — Quiero un boleto a...

When Things Just Don't Make Sense

On occasion, you may feel like not talking to anybody at all, have trouble remembering things, or find it difficult to express yourself. In such a situation, it might be wise to recite these time-tested masterpieces of misunderstanding in Spanish:

I don't speak Spanish — No hablo español

Do you speak English? — ¿Hablas inglés?

I don't understand — No entiendo

Can you speak more slowly, please? — ¿Puede hablar más despacio, por favor?

CHAPTER THREE

PACKING LIST: THE ULTIMATE PERU PACKING LIST FOR WOMEN AND MEN (INCLUDING WINTER!)

Clothing is the most fundamental item, so let's begin there. How would you describe your attire for each of the aforementioned pursuits? In fact, we went to Peru in May, right in the middle of the dry season. The weather in Peru is notoriously unpredictable, so it's best to be prepared for everything.

Depending on where you're going in Peru, here is what men and women should bring along for their wardrobe needs.

Women's Basics for Everywhere

- 2 basic bras
- 2 sports bras
- 7 pairs of underwear
- 4 pairs socks (for Keds or sneakers)
- 1 pair of Keds or comfortable and stylish walking shoes
- 2 pairs of pajamas
- 1 bathing suit (you never know if you want to go swimming in a hotel pool)
- 1 pair of sunglasses
- 1 dirty laundry bag

Men's Basics for Everywhere

- 7 pairs of underwear
- 2 pairs of pajamas
- 4 pairs of normal socks (for loafers or sneakers)

- 1 pair of loafers or comfortable walking shoes
- 1 bathing suit
- 1 pair of sunglasses
- 1 dirty laundry bag

Lima Packing List

Lima has unusually moderate weather due to the Humboldt Current, despite Peru's proximity to the Equator. Surprisingly, Lima is a mostly arid coastal city. What follows is a packing list that is quite comparable to what one would use for moderate spring or summer weather in the United States.

In addition, Limanos know how to dress chicly. For example, on a 70ºF (21ºC) day, it is very usual to wear scarves and coats, which seems absurd to us Clevelanders.

Women's Packing List for Lima

- 1-2 cute and lightweight dresses (depending on the length of stay) or 1-2 tops and 1 pair of jeans
- 1 scarf
- 1 long-sleeve sweater (if it is chilly)

- **Men's Packing List for Lima**
- 1 pair of jeans or 1 pair of shorts
- 1-2 shirts (depending on the length of stay)

Cusco Packing List (Or Other High-Altitude Cities)

Because of its greater elevation, Cusco has a completely different climate than Lima. Warm clothes for Cusco should be among your Peruvian travel essentials.

No matter the season, you can expect daytime highs of 66–70ºF (19–21ºC) and lows of 33–45ºF (1–7ºC). If you're wearing less at night, it's probably because you're more comfortable during the day.

Women's Packing List for Cusco

- 1 pair of jeans (same as Lima)

- 2-3 basic tops to mix and match (depending on the length of stay)
- 1 cute top for a nicer dinner, like at Gaston Acurio
- 1 scarf (same as in Lima)
- 1 jacket (I love the jackets from The North Face that can zip to just a lightweight raincoat or heavy jacket)

Men's Packing List for Cusco

- 1 pair of jeans (same as in Lima)
- 2-3 basic shirts (depending on the length of stay)
- 1 polo or collared shirt if going to a nicer dinner
- 1 quarter zip
- 1 jacket

Amazon Rainforest Packing List

We began our Peruvian adventure in Lima and then spent four days in the Amazon, where the heat was unbearable, until we arrived in Cusco, where the temperature was much more tolerable. The temperature in the Amazon Rainforest is rather high.

In Peru's Amazon Rainforest, daytime highs range from 85 to 91 degrees Fahrenheit (29 to 33 degrees Celsius) and nighttime lows from 64 to 72 degrees Fahrenheit (18 to 22 degrees Celsius).

But before you decide to limit yourself to shorts and t-shirts, give it some more thought. Insects, especially mosquitoes, may be rather persistent. Lightweight, long-sleeved clothes with plenty of insect repellent are a good idea, even if the daytime temperatures may get rather high.

Because it is a jungle, you should also be prepared for rain. Even though we were really fortunate that May was not a particularly rainy month, it is wise to have rain gear just in case.

Women's Packing List for the Peruvian Amazon

- 3 pairs of Merino wool hiking socks (merino wool is perfect for tucking your pants into for hiking in the forest AND it is sweat-wicking)

- 1 pair of hiking boots
- 2 pairs of leggings or hiking pants
- 3 long-sleeve lightweight, sweat-wicking tops

- 1 pair of sandals or flip flops for the lodge
- 2 pairs of comfortable shorts for the lodge
- 2 pairs of t-shirts
- 1 hat (if you wear hats)
- Use the raincoat part of your jacket

Men's Packing List for the Peruvian Amazon

- 3 pairs Merino wool hiking socks
- 1 pair of hiking boots
- 2 pairs of hiking pants
- 3 long-sleeve sweat-wicking shirts
- 2 pairs of t-shirts
- 2 pairs of shorts for the lodge
- 1 pair of sandals for the lodge
- 1 hat
- 1 raincoat (use the outer shell of the jacket)

Machu Picchu, Sacred Valley, and Rainbow Mountain Packing List

Instead of completing a full-blown hike, we opted for a 2-day/1-night trip to Machu Picchu and the Sacred Valley. I will also provide a brief rundown of other items to bring on a hiking trip. Since many businesses provide camping gear and related items, it should be very comparable.

Despite being at a lower elevation than Cusco, Machu Picchu and the Sacred Valley may still be somewhat cold, so make sure to pack appropriately. Fahrenheit (13-24 °C) is the typical temperature range throughout the year. Keep in mind that it might rain heavily, so bring appropriate rain gear.

One other thing: Rainbow Mountain may be rather chilly. One may even see snowfall. Thus, you should undoubtedly bring the necessary items. We embarked on our June walk in subzero temperatures, so we layered up heavily.

Women's Packing List for Machu Picchu, the Sacred Valley, and Rainbow Mountain

- Hiking boots and socks (from Amazon Rainforest)
- 1 pair of really warm leggings or 1 pair of thermals to go under 1 pair of hiking pants.
- 2 long sleeve sweat-wicking shirts (from Amazon Rainforest)
- 1 thermal hoodie (I love my winter running hoodie)
- 1 jacket (use the jacket with the thermal underneath)
- 1 pair of gloves
- 1 pair of earmuffs
- 1 hat (from Amazon Rainforest)

Men's Packing List for Machu Picchu, Sacred Valley, and Rainbow Mountain

- Hiking boots and socks (from Amazon Rainforest)
- 2 pairs of hiking pants (from Amazon Rainforest). Chris didn't wear thermals under his and was fine, but if you want to, pack 1-2 thermals.
- 2 long sleeve sweat-wicking shirts (from Amazon Rainforest)
- 1 quarter zip (from Cusco)
- 1 jacket (use the jacket with the thermal underneath)
- 1 pair of gloves

What to Wear if Multi-Day Trekking in Peru

This shouldn't be too different, as most of the time the company you will probably go with has the essentials already available, but just in case, here is an idea of what to bring

- Hiking boots and socks
- 1-2 pairs of thermals for under your hiking pants or thermal leggings
- Waterproof bags

- Camping gear (should be provided)
- Walking sticks (may be provided)

Toiletries to Pack for Peru

So now that you know what to wear in Peru, it is time to think about what to pack for getting ready in the morning.

Women's Toiletry Packing List for Peru

- Pads/tampons/cup. It's not that pads and tampons can't be found in Peru (I was lucky enough to start my period at the end of our trip and totally forgot to pack some), but if you have a preference for brand back home, just bring some with you.
- Deodorant
- Brush
- Travel safe straightener or curling iron
- Any makeup or under 100ml facial/hair products. I love Bumble & Bumble's All-Style hair cream.

Men's Toiletry Packing List for Peru

Deodorant

Any additional under 100ml facial/hair products. Chris tames his mane with Tresemme hair spray. It's no Steve "the hair" Harrington, but it's pretty great.

Toiletry Packing List for Both

- Shampoo, conditioner, and soap. Forget this if staying in hotels.
- Face wash and face lotion
- Razor
- Teeth stuff: floss, toothpaste, and toothbrush
- Insect Repellant. We love Badger Balm. It's all-natural, DEET free, and it works.

- Whether you're in the Amazon or hiking at high altitudes, the sun can be crazy so bring a good sunscreen.
- Condoms
- Cloth face masks for the plane (you'll thank me later)

- Sleeping mask
- Hand sanitizer

First Aid Kit to Bring to Peru

If you're going trekking, eating street food, etc., it's important to have a first-aid kit with you on your trip. What we brought along on our journey is this:

- Medicines to pack for Peru
- OTC pain reliever/fever reducer
- Antacid
- Anti-diarrheal
- Laxative
- Allergy medicine
- Motion sickness medicine
- Cough drops
- Emergen-C tablets

Other First-Aid Items to Pack for Peru

- Bandages
- Gauze
- Surgical tape
- Antibiotic ointment
- Hydrocortisone cream
- Antiseptic wipes
- Tweezers

- We were able to fit everything into a smaller bag the size of a cosmetic case, even if it seemed like a lot. All of the medications were stored in little Ziploc bags, with the exception of the prescription medications, which were retained in their original containers.

Gadgets to Bring to Peru

- Be sure you include the following items in your Peruvian packing list:
- Our beloved, compact, and user-friendly Nikon Coolpix is always at our side, along with its charger and memory cards.
- You may choose not to bring the GoPro, charger, and memory cards.
- Telephone and power adapter.
- For first-light treks: a battery-operated headlamp (unless you invest in a rechargeable one)
- Tablet and power adapter
- Adapters for travel
- wallet that blocks RIFD
- Baggage: Travelon Anti-Theft or Daylite Sling
- Viewing the Amazon Rainforest with Binoculars
- Security for your bag
- Using packing cubes to maintain order

The Official Stuff to Pack for Peru

- Don't forget to pack these official items for your trip to Peru.
- Passport
- Copies of passport, ID, travel insurance, tickets and confirmations, and itinerary

CHAPTER FOUR

GETTING AROUND IN PERU - A GUIDE FOR GETTING AROUND IN THE CITY

As a result of its position between the Atlantic Ocean, the Amazon Rainforest, and the Andes Mountains that span the length of the country, Peru is a mosaic of diverse landscapes and ecosystems.

Although Peru's varied landscape makes the country an interesting tourist destination, it also presents unique navigational challenges. Most aircraft need a connection via Lima, the capital city, and there are few paved highways connecting districts. The railway network is also poor. Traveling throughout this nation is an experience unlike any other, so don't let the logistics put you off. Our Peruvian travel guide is here.

Buses and colectivos

There are several bus alternatives in Peru. The Peruvian bus system is quite efficient, and tickets may often be purchased up to one day in advance or even on the day of departure. You should anticipate a little increase in price if you choose to work with an agent, since their primary motivation is to earn a commission. Always purchase straight from the bus company at their terminal office for the lowest fare.

Local, inexpensive buses don't stop at the main terminal but rather depart from their own offices. Typically, a single route is operated by local bus operators between any two cities. Find out which local bus stops you need to go to if you're looking for the most budget-friendly choice and are okay with the bus making frequent stops. The price of a two-hour bus ride might be as low as ten pence. Peruvian Nuevo Soles (PEN) is discussed in the note at the conclusion.

A number of major bus companies also run routes throughout the nation and even into South America. As one might expect from a low-cost carrier, they provide comfortable, allocated seats and a host of other services. One is a mechanism for passengers to check their bags, which gives them peace of mind. Your passport and expensive possessions should never be left behind, regardless of whether your luggage was checked or not.

There is usually a daytime and a nighttime option for major enterprises that operate on schedule. Even if taking the bus at night would save you money compared to staying in a hotel, taking the bus during the day will provide you with better views of the countryside. Cruz del Sur, Oltursa, Tepsa, Civa, and Movil are the principal companies. Peru Hop and Bolivia Hop are two distinct companies in Peru and Bolivia. Unlike the aforementioned bus companies, this one is specifically created to transport tourists to popular tourist spots. If you want to see the sights of Bolivia and Peru, this is the way to go as well.

Buses that operate inside a city are known as colectivos. Colectivo is another name for city buses that go to suburbs or other adjacent towns. These might take the form of a van or a real bus. The majority have names instead of numbers, and the side panels depict the major streets or communities they serve. You can always find the price listed inside the car, which ranges from S/1 to S/4. Someone other than the driver is in charge of collecting the fare. On occasion, it is asked for when you get on, but more often, it is required when you get off.

Peru by train

Trains have it tough in Peru because of the vast expanse of either the muddy Amazon rainforest or the high Andes mountains. For the most convenient rail travel, go south of Peru or along the coast around Lima. Much of southern Peru consists of high-altitude plains, known as the Altiplano, and the shoreline is mainly flat. Passengers are kindly asked to be at the station thirty minutes prior to the departure time of any train.

The most well-traveled rail route serves Aguas Calientes, the town immediately below Machu Picchu. While some trains depart from Cusco, the majority of tourists board trains in the Sacred Valley, namely from Ollantaytambo. Both PeruRail and InkaRail sell tickets. The fact that they are all controlled by the same corporation serves only to provide the appearance of market competition. In reality, the firm has a monopoly and sets very high prices. However, unless you're up for a lengthy hike, the only way to get to Machu Picchu is by rail. Roads do not exist.

The 14-hour journey to Huancayo on the Ferrocarril Central Andino is the way to get inland from Lima. The train crosses 58 bridges and passes through 69 tunnels because of the Andes' geology. Passengers have the opportunity to purchase meals and souvenirs during the break at San Bartolomé prior to continuing on with the journey. You may also take a separate train south to Huancavelica from Huancayo.

From Cusco to Puno, the Altiplano may be best explored by rail. This service, like the train to Machu Picchu, is expensive and geared toward tourists from other countries. With Puno as your jumping-off point, you may explore the Peruvian islands in Lake Titicaca and reach the Uros floating islands more easily than from any of the other cities in the region. The islands of Amantan and Taquile may be best reached from Juliaca, from which you can also visit them. There is just one airport in the area, so flying to Juliaca is your best bet.

Steaming through the Peruvian peaks on a train is an alluring prospect, but the experience isn't always as good as it seems. While certain trains are solely open to tourists and others to residents, in general, there are three different ticket classifications.
The basic economic trains are notoriously unpleasant due to their constant crowding. Enhanced security, restaurant carriages, and wait staff are available with the more costly options. Peruvian train travel is more promoted as an adventure than a means of transportation. You should not make train travel a major component of your itinerary, although it is worth checking out.

Domestic flights

The most convenient method to explore this geographically varied nation is via plane. Most planes travel via Lima since Peru is quite centrally located. From Cusco, you may take one of the few domestic direct flights to either Puerto Maldonado or Arequipa.

As more and more Peruvians travel domestically, budget airlines are vying for market share. Even the largest airline in the area, LATAM, has seen price cuts as a result of this rivalry. There are instances when flying is quicker and costs less than taking the bus.

Before booking a flight with a low-cost airline, make sure you check their track record. Having said that, I have flown domestically several times in Peru and have never had any problems beyond the usual airline delays.

Getting around by boat

Only by boat can one reach the vast majority of the Peruvian Amazon, a unique region of the biggest rainforest in South America. Most people who go to the rainforest do so via one of two airports: Iquitos or Puerto Maldonado. The whole journey from that point on will be accomplished on waterways that flow into the Amazon.

Tours of the forest and stays at lodges may be arranged via any number of local and international travel operators. Transportation by boat is a component of all of their offerings. Towns like Puerto Maldonado and Iquitos provide boat captains and guides for those who want to cruise alone. Be sure to inspect the boat for any safety gear and inquire as to the captain's experience on that specific river section.

Just so you know, mining in the Peruvian Amazon is a hotly debated topic, and there are regular demonstrations against it. Before visiting Amazon, be sure to verify with your local news outlet. You may wish to rethink your plans if there are strikes or demonstrations in the region you want to visit.

Another location accessible by boat is Lake Titicaca. From Capachica town to Amantaní island, residents may take a ferry boat for less than S/10 per person. Boats can travel from Puno to the floating Uros islands, Taquile, and Amantan. Before purchasing a ticket for the boat from Puno, it is crucial to do your research on the tour operator because they arrange the boats. While some tour operators may offer island accommodations as part of their packages, you can easily arrange transportation to the islands and stay anywhere you choose once you are there.

Renting a car in Peru

Even though my only experience with auto rentals is driving down the coast from Lima, I would definitely hire one again to see more of the nation. While renting a vehicle in Peru might be a budget-friendly option, be sure your insurance policy covers damage to the rental automobile. When customers return their rented cars, local businesses and foreign franchises in Peru often inflate the damage to make as much money as possible off of them. Because the traffic in Lima is so bad, I suggest using a cab instead of driving.

Always be aware that Peruvian police may set up roadblocks in regions where they think drug trafficking or other illicit activities are taking place if you are traveling across Peru. You will be escorted out of the car promptly if you comply courteously with their demands to search it. The narcotraffickers may periodically put up roadblocks, particularly in the northern region of Peru along the border with Colombia; therefore, it's best to only stop and roll down windows for uniformed police.

In Peru, speed bumps are strategically placed to deter drivers from exceeding the posted speed limit. Avoid driving at night and practice defensive driving. Keep in mind that the sun sets fast in Peru because of its proximity to the equator. Make it to your destination by 6 o'clock in the evening.

When I preferred not to adhere to the strict timetables of buses or airlines, or when I wanted to stop along the route, I leased a vehicle with a driver to go from city to city. Consider hiring a cab driver for the day if you'd rather not deal with driving yourself but would need more freedom than buses. Assuming everyone pitches in, the price per person drops significantly.

Taxis and rideshares

Taking a cab in Peru is easy and won't break the bank. Because of its immense size and notoriously bad traffic, Lima is home to the world's most costly taxis. There is generally a fixed tariff for the downtown area of smaller towns. To find out how much a cab ride should cost, inquire at your hotel. Travelers would be well advised to follow the Peruvians' lead and inform cab drivers of their destination and desired fare before hopping in. Not all taxis in smaller towns have the appropriate signae. It can be annoying at first, but every motorist trying to hail a ride will do it. Official taxis have prominent labels and display the driver's license and picture ID on the inside. Where I am situated in Cusco, I would gladly get in a vehicle that stops for me, regardless of whether or not it has a clearly visible taxi sign. It is recommended to wait for an official taxi if you are not acquainted with the area or if you do not understand Spanish.

Lima is one of the few places in Peru where rideshare applications like Uber are widely utilized. Passengers prefer using applications that provide information about the driver before hopping in, especially because security is a big concern in many parts of Lima. An app may also assist you in getting a fair price if you are not comfortable bargaining in Spanish.
Always shut the window, lock the door, and put your belongings at your feet while riding in a cab or automobile in Lima. Thieves posing as motorcyclists have started stealing from open cab windows at an alarming rate.

For trips between places that are rather far apart, you may also hail a cab, as indicated before. A single seat in a taxi may be reserved, or the whole vehicle might be reserved and hired out. There is usually more than one company offering intercity taxi service, and each one uses a specific street to pick up passengers. When I need a vehicle, I normally compare costs from two or three different firms to see which one has the most available space. My patience will be spared if there is just one available seat; otherwise, I will patiently wait for others to arrive.

CHAPTER FIVE

WHERE TO STAY IN PERU: BEST AREAS AND NEIGHBORHOODS TO VISIT

Due to its breathtaking landscapes and world-renowned attractions, the South American country of Peru is on the travel wish lists of many. Lima and Arequipa are two of Peru's most intriguing towns, and the country is also home to ancient sites like Chan Chan and the lost Incan metropolis of Machu Picchu. Additionally, the South Pacific coastline is home to beach resorts, while the Andes are home to mountain resorts. Stay at one of these incredible Peruvian properties every night to relax, no matter what else you do on your next South American vacation.

Hotel Isla Suasi

Located on a secluded island in Lake Titicaca, the stone-built Isla Suasi hotel complex pays homage to traditional Peruvian architecture. Because there are only 24 rooms on the whole property, each visitor will have their very own balcony with a view of the lake. Guests of the hotel have the option of lounging on the patio with a drink or two while taking in the views of Lake Titicaca, or they may arrange an exciting excursion with the helpful staff.

Aranwa Sacred Valley Hotel

Situated on the banks of the Río Vilcanota River, the Aranwa Sacred Valley Hotel & Wellness currently occupies a hacienda that dates back to the 17th century. The hotel provides all the necessities for a relaxing holiday, even if there is a lot to do in the area. The four on-site bars, art gallery, museum, movie theater, and swimming pools will undoubtedly be to your liking. While you relax and indulge in some pampering, you can take in the breathtaking scenery from the expansive spa.

Tambo del Inka

Located in the charming village of Urubamba, the Tambo del Inka Resort and Spa offers fantastic accommodations for anyone planning a visit to the Sacred Valley of the Incas. With its unrivaled setting only a short stroll from the Plaza de Armas's cafés and nightlife, Tambo del Inka is the perfect place to enjoy views of the Vilcanota River and Ch'iqun Mountain. Guests may enjoy modern Peruvian cuisine at the hotel's stylish Andean restaurant, which also has marble bathrooms, private balconies, a spa, a gaming area, and more.

Skylodge Adventure Suites

Near Cuzco, at the Skylodge excitement suites, you'll find the best combination of lodging and excitement. Transparent capsules suspended an astonishing 300 meters (1,000 feet) above the Sacred Valley floor make these unique apartments unlike anything else on Earth. This hotel will stay with you forever; getting there requires a trek or a zipline. The views of the valley below during the day and the stars at night are really breathtaking.

Belmond Miraflores Park, Lima

Located in Lima, Peru's biggest city and capital, the Belmond Miraflores Park Hotel offers a luxurious stay for travelers. Guests may enjoy breathtaking views from the posh hotel, which is located near the Larcomar clifftop retail district. Guests have the option to choose a window view that overlooks the expansive Lima metropolis below or the serene Pacific Ocean. Return to the hotel for a rejuvenating spa treatment, dinner at one of the on-site international fine dining establishments, or a swim in the outdoor pool after a day of exploring or shopping.

Sumaq Machu Picchu Hotel

The Sumaq Machu Picchu Hotel is conveniently located within twenty minutes of the famous archaeological site of Machu Picchu, as its name implies. The traditional Andean cross, which incorporates the elements of fire, water, earth, and air, served as an inspiration for the hotel. The accommodations are large and luxurious, and the restaurant provides delicious traditional Peruvian cuisine. Plus, the top apartments come with balconies where you can take in the breathtaking scenery of the Urubamba River and the mountains in the distance.

Inkaterra Reserva Amazonica

Travelers who want to explore the Amazon often stop at Puerto Maldonado, a city where the Tambopata and Madre de Dios Rivers meet. An excellent option for city lodgings, Inkaterra Reserva Amazónica blends eco-friendly architecture and facilities with opulent comforts. Each of the resort's 35 rustic wooden cabanas takes design cues from traditional Ese'Eja art and architecture. The tree canopy bridge is a must-see attraction; it allows visitors to stroll amid the trees while taking in the breathtaking scenery, fauna, and melodies of the birds.

Katari Hotel, Arequipa

Located in the middle of Arequipa, a city renowned for its three volcanoes and its astonishingly maintained architecture, the Katari Hotel offers boutique accommodations. The Katari Hotel has one of the best locations in Arequipa, facing the majestic Arequipa Cathedral and providing views of the surrounding mountains. It's hard to think of a more ideal setting for a hotel in this city. Guests of the Katari Hotel in Arequipa will enjoy colonial-style furnishings with an unexpected and historically rich touch of luxury, thanks to the hotel's exposed brick flooring and alpaca wool fabrics.

Casa Cartagena Hotel, Cuzco

Because of its closeness to Machu Picchu and its many examples of colonial architecture, Cuzco attracts many tourists. Staying the night at the famous Casa Cartagena Hotel is the best way to really appreciate the colonial architecture. The remains of the Qurikancha Temple, built in the 15th century, and the Cuzco Cathedral, built in the 16th century, are both within a short distance of Casa Cartagena, a genuine colonial house. Even though the hotel has an old-world colonial vibe, it has all the contemporary conveniences, including an indoor pool and free wireless Internet.

Hotel Paracas

Paracas is an incredible natural preserve on the southern coast of Peru. It has beautiful beaches and you can even go to nearby islands. If you're looking for a five-star hotel with water views in the area, look no further than Hotel Paracas. The Hotel Paracas offers a variety of amenities to enhance your visit, including two swimming pools, a spa, and two outstanding restaurants.

Inkaterra Machu Picchu Pueblo Hotel

Luxurious and conveniently located near the Machu Picchu train station, this boutique hotel takes design cues from its natural setting. The Inkaterra's lodgings are designed in a village style, resulting in a collection of smaller structures instead of a single ostentatious one. Indulge in a delectable meal at one of the hotel's two restaurants—a quaint thatched café with views of the Vilcanota River or a glitzy spot with views of the Urubamba River—while you're there. The hotel's villas come with five-star amenities, including butler service, private patios, plunge pools, and more.

CHAPTER SIX

BEST LUXURY HOTELS IN PERU

The Miraflores Park Hotel, Miraflores District, Lima

Many consider the Miraflores Park Hotel, located in the middle of Lima's hippest neighborhood, to be among the city's best five-star establishments. The Miraflores Park Hotel may not be as exclusive as the neighboring J.W. Marriott and Hilton, but its vantage point over the Pacific Coastline is what really makes it stand out.

The Orient Express Group owns this Lima hotel, which offers a pleasant night's stay with all the necessities and more. Just a short stroll away from the hotel are two of Lima's finest dining establishments, Astrid & Gaston and Central Restaurant, as well as the massive LarcoMar entertainment complex. But if you'd rather not go out too far at night, Mesa 18, the hotel's restaurant, is widely considered to provide some of the city's finest Peruvian-Japanese fusion cuisine. A stay at this hotel should be the first stop on any high-end Peruvian vacation package.

El Monasterio Hotel, Cusco

Despite stiff competition from newer hotels in Cusco, the Monasterio Hotel remains a popular choice due to its historic status as one of the city's premier hotels and its endearing personality. In 2009, the hotel was chosen as the best hotel in South America by the readers of Condé Nast Traveler, a US publication.

J.W. Marriott, Cusco

One of the most highly anticipated new luxury hotels in Cusco, the J.W. Marriott, opened its doors to the public for the first time in 2012. One of the best colonial hotels in Cusco, the J.W. Marriott, reportedly took over six years to finish and cost over eighty million dollars. Constructed on the foundation of the once-struggling San Agustin Convent, which dates back to the 16th century, the structure underwent a meticulous restoration process that included repairing, cleaning, and preserving its original elements. Completely renovated, the 160-room hotel now boasts an exquisite blend of religious Spanish heritage and contemporary luxury hotel comforts.

The hotel's focal point is an interior courtyard with 500 square meters (5,400 sq ft) of cloistered space. A little museum was established during the hotel's renovation and is located in the basement. Excavated artifacts and the ancient Inca and colonial muros (walls) are on display for visitors.

Tambo del Inka Resort & Spa, Urubamba, the Sacred Valley

Located in the very center of the Inca Sacred Valley, the newly constructed Tambo del Inka hotel is part of the prestigious Starwood Hotel Group that extends across the world. Part of "The Luxury Collection," this hotel is among the most prestigious in all of the Inca Sacred

Valley. Guests of the newly built Tambo del Inka hotel may enjoy a quiet, luxurious getaway from the city's noise and chaos.

The two-story stone open fireplace in the lobby is a striking contrast to the rest of the hotel's earthy tones, which are warm and welcoming. The resort has its own private train station that leads directly to Machu Picchu, a heated pool that extends outside, and a state-of-the-art fitness center and spa. Incorporate this hotel into your Peru vacation plans if you want to feel authentic Peruvian hospitality; you won't regret it.

Inkaterra Machu Picchu Hotel, Machu Picchu Pueblo

A rare find among the many five-star hotels in the area around the historic Inca fortress of Machu Picchu, the Inkaterra Machu Picchu sits within eleven acres of verdant cloud forest gardens. At this hotel, attention to detail is what really defines luxury, rather than the display of it. Some of the hotel's interesting features include a network of nature paths, a coffee and tea plantation on the premises, a refuge for the endangered spectacled bear, and the biggest private collection of orchids in South America. Thick alpaca blankets, fireplaces that crackle, and spa-style baths are all part of the cozy, unpretentious accommodations.

Suites with more space include their own gardens, bathrooms, and even plunge pools. A few suites even include a minibar and a big, cozy couch positioned beside a panoramic window that looks out into your very own tropical garden.

Choosing a hotel in Peru to serve as your home base while you discover this vast South American treasure trove is the last step in planning your dream vacation. Boutique hotels in Peru nowadays are a thriving and diverse affair, catering to all types of tourists, all because of the fast growth of the tourism sector in the last few decades.

There is no shortage of beautiful, well-appointed boutique hotels to stay in as you explore the historic Inca Trail, relax on the beautiful beaches of northern Peru, or get lost in the vibrant streets of Lima. Presented below, in no particular sequence, are a selection of the best boutique hotels in Peru, ranging from lavish colonial estates and hidden nature treasures to cutting-edge urban hotspots.

Casa Del Sol Machu Picchu

Among the most picturesque Andean locations is Casa Del Sol Machu Picchu, which is nestled next to the lively Vilcanota River. This boutique hotel is perfect for intrepid travelers planning to

visit Peru's most popular tourist attraction, Machu Picchu, thanks to its gorgeous location in the town at the base of the Inca Trail.
Rooms at Casa Del Sol range from single to triple occupancy and are furnished in a rustic manner that pays homage to the region's ancient Andean traditions. An alcoholic beverage, bathrobe, slippers, and hair dryer are all part of the welcome package for each guest. Digital safes, flat-screen TVs, and magnetic card locking systems are also available in the room.

Casa Del Sol Machu Picchu has a trendy restaurant with traditional Peruvian cuisine, an arranged shuttle to the Inca Trail, and a full breakfast buffet. The K'intu Spa is the icing on the cake of this luxurious hotel. Here, clients may unwind with a variety of treatments, such as cocoa leaf exfoliation, purifying with Inca stones, and aromatherapy facials. Near the Inca Trail and Machu Picchu, in a verdant natural location.

Casa Andina Hotels

After more than 15 years in business, Casa Andina has become one of the most well-known hotel chains in Peru. It features three distinct brands, each providing a pleasant and welcoming experience to its guests: Standard (clean, comfortable rooms with central locations), Select (modern hotels with additional facilities), and Premium (upmarket accommodations with extra particular attention to detail).

From the bustling capital of Lima to the picturesque coastal towns of Zorrito Tumbe and Piura, Casa Andina's luxury hotel brand has over 20 sites in all the main tourist destinations. Rooms at each of these hotels are light and airy, equipped with contemporary conveniences, and accompanied by friendly, multilingual concierges. Casa Andina hotels also have hip eateries with creative menus that mix contemporary flavors with classic Peruvian dishes. Offering a wide range of accommodations in various areas of Peru, with a solid reputation for reliability.

Esplendor Cusco

One of the best boutique hotels in the old Inca city, Esplendor Cusco, is located only a few steps from the historic Plaza de Armas and the lively San Pedro market. Located in a charming colonial-style structure, this five-star hotel offers 24 spacious rooms with contemporary furnishings, hardwood floors, and subdued color palettes.

A coffee maker, minibar, closet, and free Wi-Fi are included in every room. Relax on one of the sun-kissed seats in the expansive courtyard, one of the most picturesque aspects of Esplendor Cusco, after a day of touring. Enjoy complimentary breakfast at Esplendor Cusco, the hotel's on-site restaurant, and relax in the hotel's luxurious hot tub. Airport transportation, massages, and dry cleaning are available at an additional fee to visitors. Conveniently located near Cusco's top attractions, with contemporary decor and cozy accommodations.

Peru Star Boutique Apartment Hotel

Located in the prime San Isidro neighborhood of Lima, the family-run Peru Star Boutique Apartment Hotel offers comfortable accommodations in a stylish setting. Located on a peaceful residential street, it offers a tranquil escape from the bustle of the city center, making it the perfect alternative for those interested in seeing the Peruvian capital.

The large, comfortable rooms include colorful furnishings and plush mattresses, creating a homey atmosphere. Comfy couches, flat-screen TVs, and minibars are standard in all of the rooms. For those seeking the height of relaxation in absolute luxury, Peru Star also has duplex, superior double, and double apartments.

If you're planning a trip with your four-legged buddy, this hotel is a great choice since it allows pets. Ceviche, lomo saltado, and aji de gallina are just a few of the classic Peruvian delicacies available at the on-site restaurant, which also provides a complimentary continental breakfast.

Terra Andina Colonial Mansion

Guests of this magnificent hotel may step inside a magnificent colonial palace and experience what it was like to live in medieval Cusco. In addition, the San Pedro Market, San Pedro Church, and Plaza de Armas—three of Cusco's most famous landmarks—are all within walking distance of Terra Andina. Just one kilometer away from the hotel are the ancient Inca temple ruins of Qorikancha.

The 31 rooms in this luxurious structure all have private bathrooms, cable TVs, and fine Peruvian cotton linens. The decor is simple and clean. Enjoy a king or queen bed, a minibar, and a la carte breakfast when you upgrade to a Deluxe or Superior accommodation. In addition to a sophisticated cocktail bar, in-room massages, airport transfers, and tour packages of Cusco and the surrounding area are available at Terra Andina.

Dine on Andean specialties with a gourmet touch at Terra Andina's rustic restaurant, which has travertine tables and iron-wrought seats. In the middle of Cusco's old center, with breathtaking architecture and an excellent restaurant.

This concludes our rundown of the five top boutique hotels in Peru. During your Peruvian adventures, you may relax in the lap of luxury at one of these verdant hotels that is conveniently located near all of the country's most popular sites. You may experience the pinnacle of comfort and hospitality at any of these Peruvian hotels, thanks to their prime locations, cutting-edge facilities, and first-rate service.

There are a variety of hotels in Machu Picchu to choose from, ranging from affordable to quite luxurious, so be sure to research your options before your trip.

BEST CHEAP AND MID-RANGE HOTELS IN PERU

HOTEL RESIDENCIAL CARLOS

Since this motel was just meant to serve as a stopover, its selection was based on its affordability. But for the next morning's bus, I double-checked that it wasn't too far away. Lastly, I would like to mention that the reception was excellent and the rooms were accurate and tidy.

HOSTAL CURASI

Reasonable pricing and a prime position (between the oasis and the dunes) were the deciding factors in my choice of this facility. An additional perk was the use of a stunning pool with a picturesque outlook. My recommendation is this.

EL PATIO DE ELISA

Thomas, our local contact, really suggested this hotel, and I listened. The location is ideal, and the pricing is right, too. Its central location in downtown Arequipa made it easy for us to go anywhere we wanted to go, whether it was sightseeing, dining, or shopping. The setting is just perfect! On top of that, I loved having breakfast on the patio. As far as I'm concerned, it's the finest. reasonable Arequipa hotel rate.

HOSTAL VIRGEN DE LAS NIEVES

Always considering the area while making my choices, this little motel is a part of it. It takes only a few minutes to travel by boat to the islands in Lake Titicaca.

Not only are the rooms cramped, but the hotel itself is quite loud. However, everyone had a wonderful time! They gave us an unbelievable deal on a two-day trip to Lake Titicaca. They deliver delicious breakfasts at the time you choose, even if that's really early in the morning. Lastly, it has Wi-Fi, which is the cherry on top! Therefore, it's not awful considering the price.

CHEZ ARNAUD

We had spoken with Arnaud Alagadec about creating the trip schedule in the days leading up to departure. This Frenchman, who lived in Cuzco for a while after marrying a Peruvian, gave us two of his apartments. I had no complaints about the spacious and cozy accommodations. However, there was a little drawback to the shared restrooms' electrical setup... On top of that, we have to use a cab to go to the city center, tourist attractions, or even just the restaurant, as the home is a little far from there. Take note that the price for the cab was just three euros! But Arnaud's hospitality, charisma, compassion, and invaluable advice make him an excellent recommendation in and of itself.

EL MISTICO MACHU PICCHU

The hotel's proximity to the Machu Picchu bus stop and its central location in Hot Waters were the two most important factors in my decision. Even though our night lasted just two hours, the room was lovely and really comfy. Apart from that, the Wi-Fi was fine, and the bus and rail stations were within a short walking distance for our return journey. End up being a great decision.

HOSPEDAJE DIMAR INN

The hotel's prime position in the vibrant and touristic MIRAFLORES sector was a major factor in its selection. The hotel is conveniently located near many nightlife venues, including pubs and restaurants. When compared to other hotels in LIMA of the same category, its pricing is reasonable, and its location is ideal for organizing sightseeing trips. It is really the best hotel plan for LIMA; I can state it again.

BEST HOSTELS IN PERU

As far as backpacking destinations go, Peru is unrivaled. From the Amazon to the Pacific, from huge deserts to the Andes, this nation is full of amazing experiences. For budget-conscious visitors like myself, it is a traveler's dream. Hostels in Peru are top-notch, with some stunning properties available at very low costs. I am really grateful to be able to afford the opportunity to spend an eternity in Peru.

These hostels were the nicest I've stayed at in Peru over my many months of traveling across the country. You won't believe this, but you can get all of them for less than $20 each night.

Wild Rover Hostel | Huacachina

I vowed to myself that I would not stay at Wild Rover in an effort to maintain my current pattern of abstaining from party hostels. However, my identity was restored to me in due time. There is no need for Mufasa to make an aerial appearance. I spent five weeks in Huaraz mostly abstaining from parties, but I gave in to the allure of the revelry at some point. I went on a bender in Lima and Huacachina right after my weeks of hiking and wholesomeness in Huaraz. Among the top party hostels in South America, Huacachina's Wild Rover is among the finest. At times, it resembles a five-star resort rather than a budget hostel—that is, until nightfall, when the bar is flooded with young travelers seeking love and a good time.

ATMA Hostel & Yoga | Huanchaco (Trujillo)

Before returning to the Andes to tackle some of the most breathtaking and difficult hikes Peru has to offer, I had intended to make a brief stay in Huanchaco. I remained at ATMA for a lot longer than intended because of the positive energy and $2 yoga lessons, even if Huanchaco doesn't really have much to offer. Have I mentioned the free-roaming tortoises and rabbits that inhabit the hostel garden? After a long day of surfing, I would often go to a hammock to cuddle with a rabbit. Huanchaco is a wonderful place to relax, and ATMA is an ideal base for doing so.

Loki | Cusco

I will always have a soft spot for Loki. Back in the day, when I was just starting out on my nomadic travels, Loki was the very first hostel I stayed at in Cusco. There were many happy times here, but I can't put my finger on most of them. A wild Loki ensues. Loki is considered by many Cusco backpackers to be one of the city's most sacred places. A trip to Cusco would be incomplete without trying one of their famous blood bombs.

Wild Rover Hostel | Cusco

Very seldom do I voluntarily ascend a terrifying slope for anything. One such spot is Wild Rover. Perched atop Cerro Santa Ana, Wild Rover offers breathtaking views of Cusco and the Andes. Unlike any other Cusco hostel, this one has a patio bar and restaurant. Not only is it one of the most reasonably priced hostels in Cusco, but it is also generally considered to be the top party hostel in the city. For anyone seeking a more sociable experience, it is an excellent option because of its inexpensive beverages, nightly gatherings, and many free shots.

Selina Miraflores, Lima

It took me a few weeks of hostel hopping in Lima before I finally gave in and booked a room at Selina, which was also in Huaraz. I figured that would be the best option in Lima. Selina is the most opulent and reasonably priced alternative among Lima's several choices for budget-conscious travelers. Its prime Miraflores location puts you in close proximity to some of Lima's top attractions. In addition, there is a library, movie theater, restaurant, café, and shared kitchen. Selina is always an excellent bargain because of all of its wonderful features.

MB Hostel (Mercaderes Backpackers) | Arequipa

Only the stunning patio with views of the city can compare to MB Hostel's prime downtown position. You can start your day off well with a coffee on their magnificent rooftop, and breakfast is already included in the already low price at MB. One of my favorite things to do in Arequipa was to relax on a hammock here at sunset. The city and mountains are best seen on sunny days. If you do decide to drop by, please tell Happy the cat that I sent you.

Pariwana Hostel, Cusco

Pariwana is one of Cusco's most popular hostels. The rationale is obvious. There is a huge outdoor plaza, a movie room, and a restaurant and bar all in one area at this roomy hostel. When it comes to hostels in Cusco, their breakfast buffet is among the finest. Pariwana has the best possible position, only two blocks from Cusco's vibrant nightlife zone and the Plaza de Armas.

Black Llama Hostel, Lima

Black Llama Hostel is right in the middle of Miraflores's party zone. My first night in Peru was at this hostel on my first ever backpacking trip all those years ago, and I've been here several times since then. Back then, it was a Kokopelli, but now they're at a Barranco mansion-style hostel. With its convenient rooftop bar and patio, Black Llama Hostel is the perfect place to unwind before a wild Lima night on the town. Bizarro, my favorite nightclub in Lima, is just around 53 seconds away on foot. I walked intoxicated out of the club, not sure how I would get home that night, but I was at the hostel in no time. I was never able to take advantage of the complimentary breakfast as I was unable to rise before midday after a night on the town in Lima.

Moksha Surf & Yoga Hostel | Huanchaco

Moksha, similar to ATMA, is all about surfing and yoga. Right in the middle of Huanchaco, Moksha is a little more central than ATMA. During the day, they provide yoga and surf instruction, and after dark, they usually turn into a passable nightclub. Moksha is constantly putting on an event where you can have a few beers and have a good time, even if Huanchaco isn't exactly renowned for its nightlife.

Pariwana Hostel, Lima

With its prime position next to Lima's lively Kennedy Park, Pariwana offers one of the city's most desirable addresses. If you're in the mood for something more authentic, the public bus station is only a few steps away and can transport you anywhere in the city. No Pariwana hostel, not even the one in Lima, ever fails to impress. The hostel's size and layout are unexpected considering its central Lima location. In fact, there's a large restaurant and bar on the premises that puts on entertaining events every night for people to gather and mingle. Most people's Peruvian journeys begin or conclude in Lima, and Pariwana is a fantastic spot to begin or depart on a high note.

CHAPTER SEVEN

11 MUST EAT PLACES IN PERU: WHERE TO EAT IN 2024

Peruvians are known for their delectable cuisine that showcases fresh ingredients from all around the nation, from the Amazon to the Andes. Incredible ceviche and fusions of South American and Asian flavors from centuries of migration make Peruvian cuisine among the world's best.

Lima, the capital, serves delectable seafood and ceviche made from fish plucked from the nearby Pacific. The Andean Mountain region's cuisine, on the other hand, is renowned for its quinoa-based meals, fresh river trout, and potato varieties. Fish cooked on banana leaves with unusual Amazonian fruit sauces is a specialty of the Amazon region, which is located deep within the country. For your dining pleasure, we have compiled a list of the top 7 restaurants in Peru.

1. **Amaz, Lima**

Stop by Amaz in Lima if you're craving some Amazonian flavors. Traditional Amazonian plantains, snails, and coconut rice are among the dishes offered. Sushi with fruity and spicy sauces is another delectable option at this eatery. To complement your dinner, try one of the unusual cocktails on the menu.

2. **Huaca, Pullana, Lima**

Huaca Pullana in Lima is situated on the site of pre-Inca ruins of the same name, so it's the perfect place to eat if you've ever desired to do so. Indulge in a mystical meal while taking in breathtaking views of the ruins from the restaurant's patio. The roasted guinea pig is a classic Peruvian meal, so don't be timid about ordering it. Aji de Gallina, a Peruvian delicacy of chicken cooked in a hot yellow pepper sauce, lobster risotto, and seabass are some of the less daring options.

3. **La Lucha Sangucheria, Lima and Arequipa**

A visit to Peru would be remiss if it didn't have a sangucheria sandwich. The major towns in Peru are teeming with sandwich businesses, contributing to the country's stellar reputation for sandwiches. You can find La Lucha restaurants in both Lima and Arequipa. The crust is beautiful and crunchy, and the bread is very fresh. Meanwhile, it's a fantastic choice for both meat eaters and vegans, and there is a plethora of tasty fillings to experiment with.

4. **Pachapapa, Cusco**

Pachapapa is a restaurant in Cusco's trendy San Blas neighborhood. It offers tasty native Andean cuisine, such as roasted guinea pig, alpaca meat skewers, and fish caught in the area. You will feel as if you have entered a local's home when you dine at this restaurant, thanks to its typical Cuzqueño décor.

5. **Salamanto Restaurante, Arequipa**

In Arequipa, you can find Salamanto Restaurante, which offers traditional food with a contemporary spin. The restaurant employs historic traditions to produce the food, creating an astonishing blend of old and contemporary. Tapas like alpaca and fish prepared with unusual sauces will wow you on the seven-or ten-course tasting menu.

6. Jardin Secreto, Cusco

Looking for a fast Andean bite? Jardin Secreto, an informal restaurant serving up indigenous food, is a fantastic choice. The menu features traditional Peruvian dishes such quinoa soups, grilled fish, and lomo saltado, a stir-fried beef dish with onions, Chile, and veggies. To set the atmosphere, listen to live Andean folk music in the evenings.

7. La Mar, Lima

Ceviche, the national dish of Peru, is an absolute must-try on any vacation to the country. La Mar, located in Lima's hip Miraflores area, is known for its delicious ceviche and upscale restaurant ambiance. The ceviche is just delicious. Chilcanos or pisco sours are perfect cocktails to accompany your dinner.

8. **Restaurant Cordano, Lima**

Cordao Restaurant has been known as "The President's Cafe" for the last century since it has provided meals to almost every president of Peru. Its ancient structure dates back to the early 1900s, and its location just across from the presidential palace makes it an ideal spot for the nation's officials to have lunch. Because it has remained almost unchanged for decades, the restaurant's atmosphere will transport diners back in time. Place an order for some traditional Peruvian fare, such as quinoa soup and lomo saltado, a stir-fried meal of beef strips.

9. Dadá, Lima

The trendy Barranco neighborhood is home to Dadá, a hipster eatery. Get a pisco sour or Chilcano fruit punch to wash down your dinner; these Peruvian drinks are legendary. Sample some of the seafood delicacies, such as spicy fried fish, seafood rice, and zesty ceviche. Delectable pizzas, priced at around $4, are also available. Featuring arty design, the restaurant is housed in a renovated colonial structure.

10. Punto Azul, Lima

For some of the city's finest ceviche and seafood, go no further than Punto Azul. Choose from shrimp fettuccine, seafood risotto, or mixed ceviche. Come hungry since the quantities are huge at this eatery! Be warned: the pisco sour drinks are really addicting. You'll be glad you waited in the often-long queue at the Miraflores location.

EAT LIKE A LOCAL IN PERU: MUST-TRY FOODS

One of the best ways to immerse yourself in Peruvian culture while traveling is to sample the local cuisine. Peru is home to a wide variety of mouthwatering meals that you won't find anywhere else. The World Travel Awards named Peru the top South American culinary destination for 2022, so now is a fantastic opportunity to visit this amazing nation and sample some authentic Peruvian cuisine.

One distinctive feature of Peruvian food is the frequent incorporation of both international and regional culinary traditions, as well as traditional ingredients that are exclusive to Peru.

Peruvian cuisine is among the most intriguing in the world because of its worldwide impact. Although Peruvian fusion cuisine is a foodie's paradise, no trip to Peru would be complete without sampling some of the country's most famous dishes in Lima, the capital city, which has an internationally acclaimed and vibrant restaurant scene.

You may learn more about the culture and history of the people you're visiting, discover new flavors, and enrich your vacation experience by dining on regional specialties. Take a peek at some of Peru's mouthwatering must-eat dishes before you set out on your Peruvian adventure.

1. **Ceviche**

As the national cuisine of Peru, the seafood salad ceviche should be at the top of every traveler's list of must-eat Peruvian dishes. Lime juice marinates cold-cooked fish, which is then served with boiling corn, sweet potatoes, red onions, and lime wedges. Peruvian ceviche differs from its Mexican counterpart in that it does not include avocado or tomatoes. Many

Peruvians believe ceviche to have aphrodisiac and hangover-curing properties because of its widespread popularity.

Actually, National Ceviche Day is celebrated annually on June 28th in Peru to honor this beloved and significant cuisine. So, if you happen to be traveling to Peru on that day, you could discover restaurants and hotels providing special menus or inventive takes on the dish to commemorate the occasion.

2. **Lomo Saltado (Beef stir-fry)**

Among the many delicious Peruvian dishes, Lomo Saltado is a must-try. This meal begins in Lima and consists of marinated sirloin steak, red onions, tomatoes, and the most crucial ingredient, a fiery pepper called Ají Amarillo, which is stir-fried. French fries and rice are the standard accompaniments.

In order to make Lomo Saltado, Chinese cooks from Lima's Chinco neighborhood began sautéing beef in a wok in the early 1800s. Although Lomo Saltado is now a national phenomenon, its origins can be traced back to Lima's Calle La Concepcion, also called Peru's Barrio Chino.

3. Pollo a la Brasa (Roasted Chicken)

Peruvians are famed for their Pollo a la Brasa, a rotisserie-roasted entire chicken. The meal comes with salad and French fries, but what really makes it special is the ají verde sauce, which is a combination of cashews, sour cream, mayonnaise, and jalapeños for a little heat.

For supper, which for Peruvians often occurs between 8 and 10 o'clock in the evening, they often consume this new cuisine. In 1950, it was first set up in the Chaclacayo neighborhood. An immigrant from Switzerland named Roger Schuler lived there for a while, and he learned chicken cooking techniques from his chef. Gather your loved ones around a plate of Pollo a la Brasa at one of Lima's several eateries serving this dish.

4. **Ají de Gallina (Creamy chicken)**

Ají de Gallina is an additional delicious chicken dish from Peruvian cuisine. It consists of shredded chicken wrapped in a thick sauce including cheese, walnuts, and Ají Amarilla sauce, which adds a fruity and spicy flavor.

This meal has been enjoyed by Peruvians since the 16th century. It is believed to have been introduced to Peru by African slaves who were sent there by the Spanish. Aji de gallina was born out of a need to find a good use for leftover chicken and potatoes.

5. **Causa (Potato Casserole)**

Served cold, this Peruvian appetiser resembles an intriguing burger. The 'buns' often include mashed potatoes and ají amarillo as their base, and they are filled with avocado, chicken, or tuna.

Some think the Quechua word kausaq, which the Incas used to call potatoes, means "sustenance for life." This lends credence to the idea that the Incas were responsible for coining the term.

6. Anticuchos (Beef heart skewers)

Never tried heart before, but would want to! If so, you will love Peruvian anticuchos. Garlic and vinegar season this tough beef-heart, which is often flash-fried for a few seconds to soften it up a little before serving. Marinated chicken kebabs are an alternative for those who do not like beef heart.

You can get anticuchos in every area of Lima, and they are best eaten while strolling about (though you can get them in restaurants, too, but they aren't authentic).

One of Peru's most popular traditional cuisines is celebrated annually on October 3rd on the "Dia Nacional del Anticucho," a national holiday.

7. **Picarones**

Picarones are the perfect on-the-go snack if you're looking for something sweet and easy. These doughnut-like snacks have a sweet and spicy flavor. Sweet potatoes and various pumpkins are the mainstays.

You can get picarones, a popular treat among Peruvians, in almost every street market in the country.

8. **Papa a la Huancaina**

Papa a la Huancaina is another appetizer that you may get in Peru. Cold cooked eggs top this spicy salad, which consists of boiled potatoes in a creamy sauce. A combination of milk, cheese, crushed crackers, and garlic makes up the bright yellow salad dressing.

In contrast to the customary sweet or acidic flavors found in salads, papa a la Huancaina is spicy.

THE 10 BEST PERU CLUBS AND BARS

There is a wide selection of bars in Lima. Lima is the perfect place for both formal evenings out and more relaxed getaways. To experience the vibrant nightlife of Lima, visit the posh Miraflores neighborhood, the artistic Barranco, or even the Historic Center.

1. **Carnaval**

Located in Lima's posh San Isidro district is Carnaval Bar. In addition to being among the top bars in Lima, Carnaval is among the top bars around the globe. Just two years after it first opened to the public in 2017, the bar was named the second best in South America and ranked thirteenth on the 2019 list of the worlds fifty finest bars.

The owner's experiences as a bartender across the globe served as inspiration for the bar's idea. He returned home with fresh, original ideas for recipes as a result of his adventures. The "Alegoria Alegria" is a refreshing drink that we highly suggest. It combines gin, elderberry liqueur, cucumber, lime, and mint. A tasting menu of seven specialty cocktails is also available for those who want a more in-depth exploration of the cocktail world. Carnaval offers a wide variety of alcoholic beverages, as well as appetizers, main courses, and desserts, all of which include a different spirit.

The inside is warm and well furnished. The idea of combining different tastes is reflected in the décor, which includes more than 800 bottles of liqueurs from all around the world.

2. **Gran Hotel Bolivar**

Located in Lima's historic district, the Gran Hotel Bolivar has a rich history. The hotel, which was opened to the public in 1924, is an iconic building in Plaza San Martin. The plaza was dedicated in 1921 to commemorate the centennial of Peru's independence, which was just a few years before. Rafael Marquina, a Peruvian architect, designed the hotel with the dual objectives of modernizing Lima and offering dignified accommodations for visiting politicians. The hotel has hosted many notable visitors, including politicians, Orson Welles, Ava Gardner, and John Wayne in the 1940s and 1950s, among others.

Despite its 1972 designation as a national monument, the hotel has seen a steady loss in popularity due to ongoing refurbishment and the emergence of other, more opulent options. Still, no trip to Lima is complete without a stop at the Gran Hotel Bolivar's cocktail bar. Along with one of Peru's largest and finest pisco sours, the Pisco Sour Catedral, it provides wonderful old-school charm.

3. **DaDA Bar**

The Barranco location of DaDA Bar is a restored colonial house. To sum it up, they transformed the colonial-style structure into a hip bar with a different theme for each area. In the warmer months, the outside patio is even more beautiful. A term borrowed from the Dadaist movement of the early 20th century. Imagine the Mona Lisa with a mustache or spectacles.

The goal of DaDA Bar is to bring together the worlds of art, culture, and cuisine. This is why the watering hole hosts a wide variety of activities, including art exhibitions, stand-up comedy, readings, concerts, and more. Their distinctive gin cocktails and gourmet pizza will transport you to Lima's bohemian nightlife.

4. **Barra 55**

Barra 55 is another Barranco watering hole, with over twenty distinct gins to choose from. The precise size of the bar—55 square meters, or around 180 square feet—is the inspiration for the name Barra 55. After a long day at the office, residents of Barranco would go to this little pub.

This pub in Lima, Peru, is considered one of the greatest due to its contemporary, Nordic-inspired design, excellent cocktails, and delicious appetizers. Gin isn't the only alcoholic beverage on the menu; rum, pisco, whiskey, craft beers, and ciders round out the drinks. They have a variety of small dishes available for nibbling, including platters of cheese and Spanish tortillas.

5. **BarBarian**

When it came to craft beer in Peru, Barbarian was an early pioneer, and it remains one of Lima's finest brewers today. In the middle of Miraflores, close to Parque Kennedy, you'll find their initial establishment. The hand-painted walls are the first thing that catches the eye when you enter their Miraflores location. Next thing you know, you'll be staring at the international beer bottle collection on the other wall. In general, it's a fantastic, lively spot to have a few beers. Twenty different craft beers are available on a rotating basis; some of them have Peruvian ingredients like quinoa and coca leaves added to them. As for the menu, you may choose from burgers, sandwiches, wings, and fries. If you want to get a seat at Barbarian, a renowned Lima nightclub, you'll have to get there early. Furthermore, Barranco is home to a second Barbarian.

6. **Juanito**

There are few pubs in Barranco as historic as Juanito. Artists and authors have frequented the pub since it first opened in 1937. Juan "Juanito" Casusol, the proprietor and namesake, passed away in 2010, ending its operation. But in 2014, after a four-year absence, the pub was re-opened by his sons. Both the delicious meal and the kind, helpful staff are major selling points. The chili and pint of beer are worth the stop.

In the event that you are still hungry after that, we suggest the tacu tacu or ají de Gallina. For a laid-back and welcoming Peruvian bar experience in Lima, Juanito is hard to beat.

7. **Ayahuasca**

The legendary Ayahuasca bar is an essential stop on any tour of Lima's top watering holes. An 1880s converted casona, Ayahuasca is located in Barranco's bohemian area. They transformed a historic estate in Republican architecture into a lively watering hole with many themed rooms. After opening in 2008, Ayahuasca quickly rose to prominence as one of Peru's most distinctive watering holes.

Peruvian pisco is a common ingredient in many of the drinks on the extensive menu. Pisco, coca leaves, aguaymanto (gooseberry), and tumbo (banana passionfruit) make up the Ayahuasca Sour, which tourists should sample. You may have a variety of foods to go along with your beverages. The typical Peruvian appetizers, including fried chicken, tequeños, and anticuchos, are our favorites. Piqueo Ayahuasca is another option.

8. Barranco Beer Company

The Barranco Beer Company is, unsurprisingly, a brewery located in the very center of Barranco. Ever since it opened in 2013, it has posed a formidable challenge to Barbarian. Indoor and outdoor seating are available in their cozy taproom, which is located on the top level. On tap at all times are four flagship beers and eleven seasonal drafts, all of which are made in-house. Also, for snacks, there's a wide selection of pizza, sandwiches, fries, and more.

9. La Destileria

Miraflores is home to the famous La Destilería bar and nightclub, which provide tasty appetizers and drinks, and in the evenings, they have DJs and live music. The pub is warm and inviting, with lovely furnishings and an antique, industrial vibe. The "La Ofrenda" cocktail—a potent blend of pisco, passionfruit, orange juice, and chicha de jora—is our favorite. La Destilería, Lima, is the best spot to enjoy the Peruvian nightlife.

10. Victoria Bar

We return to Barranco to complete our ranking of the top Lima bars. The stunning Casona Cilloniz Mansion is home to Victoria Bar. Cocktails, both traditional and creative, are available on the menu. The live DJs play a variety of music styles, including techno, jazz, and rock, and the outside terrace is the perfect place to dance. The most important thing is to have a chilcano, which is one of the most famous beverages in Peru. As you begin your exploration of Lima's nightlife, a passionfruit sour is an excellent choice.

CHAPTER EIGHT

BEST PERU BEACHES TO VISIT RIGHT NOW

The beaches of Peru are as varied as the people and cultures that inhabit them. They stretch from the northern seashore, amid arid tropical forests, to the border of the Andes, where the Humboldt Current's rich environment meets the shores.

With over 2,500 kilometers (1553 miles) of coastline, Peru is adorned with an abundance of breathtaking beaches.

PUNTA SAL

Found on the seashore in the north. Just eighty kilometers south of Tumbes, the country's northernmost city and its border with Ecuador. Among the Andean country's first-class beaches, Punta Sal is renowned for its beauty and charm. Because it is located near the equator, which causes a southward circulation of warm waters known as the "El Niño Current," the seawater temperature remains about 24 °C all year round. Punta Sal is widely regarded as one of the top beaches in the Andean nation for sport fishing due to its gentle sand, breathtaking vistas, nice weather, and placid seas.

It is one of the longest coastlines, stretching for 6.5 kilometers. You can easily enjoy it without worrying about being in close proximity to other people because of the ample space. Regardless, the rough terrain will require some walking before you can swim. Its unmatched beauty and vast littoral also draw investors and visitors. There are a wide variety of charming inns and eateries here that are perfect for a vacation in Peru. Because, in comparison to other places, Punta Sal has an excellent system of hotels.

MANCORA

Mancora is definitely the most beautiful beach in the area. This beach is one of the top locations due to its excellent beaches, large waves that are perfect for surfing, and consistently good weather. Located 187 kilometers north of Piura in Peru's hottest area, this sunny paradise welcomes visitors and residents alike all year round with its carefree vibe, powdery white beaches, warm waves, and clear blue sky.

Not only is it a popular spot for parties, but it's also famous for surfing. There may not be many people living in Mancora, but there are plenty of businesses catering to tourists, including hotels, restaurants, and resorts. One of the most popular spots for youthful tourists, this beach is also quite easy to get to. Furthermore, Máncora is home to rare marine species, making it an ideal location for scuba divers and anglers.

CABO BLANCO

Without a shadow of a doubt, Cabo Blanco ranks among Peru's finest beaches. Everyone is familiar with Ernest Hemingway, the Nobel laureate in literature, even if books aren't your thing. You should be aware that Cabo Blanco served as an inspiration for his renowned work,

"The Old Man and the Sea," if that suits you. Legend has it that Hemingway spent about ten months of the 1950s and 1960s there, when he enjoyed fishing for black marlin. However, this beach is well-known for having an ideal wave that only skilled surfers can ride. There is a window of opportunity to ride high-quality waves from November through January.

Its northerly location is in Piura, at 197 kilometers. There are waves that may be twelve feet high. Between the months of October and January, they may even make a tumultuous impact with rocks. Therefore, even if you are a seasoned surfer, you should proceed with caution.

LOBITOS

Lobitos is the place to go if you're looking for a beach with a mix of adventure and history. This site, which dates back to the late 19th century, was a historic British oil town situated 127 kilometers northwest of Piura. It was forbidden for the Peruvians to access this zone. In this sense, the Peruvian army and government expelled the British and established a military facility there in 1968.

Thus, in the mid-1990s, the military dismantled the base that had been constructed there. Passing by various derelict military installations, rusted minor refineries, and deserted Victorian apartments. So, this background is mixed with ideal waves that are almost 8 feet high. These are even listed as the best Peruvian surfing spots. Not to mention the warm weather, bright blue sky all year round, white beach, and clear, intensely blue sea. There must be a plethora of surf schools in the area.

CERRO AZUL

A Beach Boys song even made reference to the famous Cerro Azul surf. Within the San Vicente de Cañete area, 155 kilometers south of Lima, you can find its five beaches. There was a time when this port was very vital for trade. One distinctive feature of Cerro Azul is the British pier, which dates back to the early 1900s. There are many different kinds of animals, as well as pre-Incan artifacts, an abandoned lighthouse, and more. Although Cerro Azul offers a variety of attractions, it is sometimes overlooked as a summer vacation. So there won't be a lot of people there, which is great.

Jet skis, fishing, kayaking, rafting, and surfing are just a few of the many activities available. Just south of the pier are the holiday houses, in case you are intending to remain for an extended period of time. Something new to try on your next Peruvian holiday.

LAS POCITAS

Las Pocitas is located 217 kilometers north of Piura, not far from Mancora. Little Mancora and Máncora Chico are two other names for it. Compared to its elder sibling, it is a less strenuous option. There is a large range of hotels that provide sea views. The scenery and pools at some of them are out of this world. If you're a couple seeking a break from the constant festivities, this beach is perfect for you.

The white-sand beaches and turquoise seas of Pocitas provide a striking visual contrast. The unmatched allure of this vista is enhanced by the tropical gardens that surround it. At low tide, the beach becomes a wonderful platform for exploring tiny aquatic organisms. On top of that, it has all the makings of a perfect honeymoon hideaway. However, Hotel Las Pocitas is the place to go if you want a more luxurious beachfront experience. A more opulent option that will put a spell on your stay.

PLAYA ROJA

The term "Red Beach" comes from the stark contrast between the red sands of La Playa Roja and the blue water of the ocean. Giving rise to stunning landscapes worth enjoying. They were formed when old lava began to solidify in the region due to erosion. In certain spots, the beach is framed by towering cliffs, which adds to its charm. This spot is ideal for those who like natural scenery and sunsets if they are seeking things to do in Paracas. The Paracas National Reserve is home to this site, which is 82 kilometers west of Ica and about four hours away from Lima.

The area's abundance of wildlife is a direct result of its central location inside a reserve. Because of preservation efforts, a large portion of the terrain is off-limits. Not all travel agents are permitted. In order to fully appreciate all the sights, it is advised to arrange a few excursions.

PLAYA LA MINA

Tourists flock to Peru's La Mina beach, among many others. Keep in mind that it's a top choice for swimmers. From January through March, it is likely to be bustling with people enjoying the summer season. Southwest of Lima, 87 kilometers away, lies Ica. Plus, the name comes from a local coal mine that used to be there. Paracas National Reserve's most breathtaking desert scenery encircles it.

The Pacific Ocean meets breathtaking sandstone rock formations at a point where the waters sparkle with a verdant turquoise hue. Plus, when the night sky transforms into a star festival for campers and stargazers, La Mina becomes an even more breathtakingly stunning sight. Nevertheless, La Mina's waters may turn very chilly in some seasons. Therefore, summer is the ideal time to explore Peru and La Mina in particular. And maybe, just maybe, you'll be fortunate enough to see some sea lions.

ROMANTIC PLACES IN PERU: SPOTS TO WOO YOUR PARTNERS

The most romantic spots in Peru for couples, such as Paracas, Cusco, and the Sacred Valley, combine culture, adventure, and romance.

You may unwind at your leisure in the picture-perfect seaside village of Paracas, learn about colonial history in the picturesque city of Cusco, and take in breathtaking panoramas of the Sacred Valley.

If you're planning a romantic getaway to Peru, these are the top spots to visit for couples. Indulge in the delights of a private Peruvian getaway while exploring golden beaches, lush jungles, and ancient towns.

1. **Paracas**

Just south of Lima, on Peru's western coast, is this picture-perfect beach village. White-sand beaches and rocky shorelines are popular destinations for couples seeking romantic getaways in beautiful beach bungalows.

Immerse yourself in the beauty of the South Pacific Ocean as you dine at world-renowned restaurants and stay in glitzy hotels in one of the most picturesque coastal sections of the nation. In Paracas, you may take in the unparalleled splendor of the sun-kissed coastline by foot or boat.

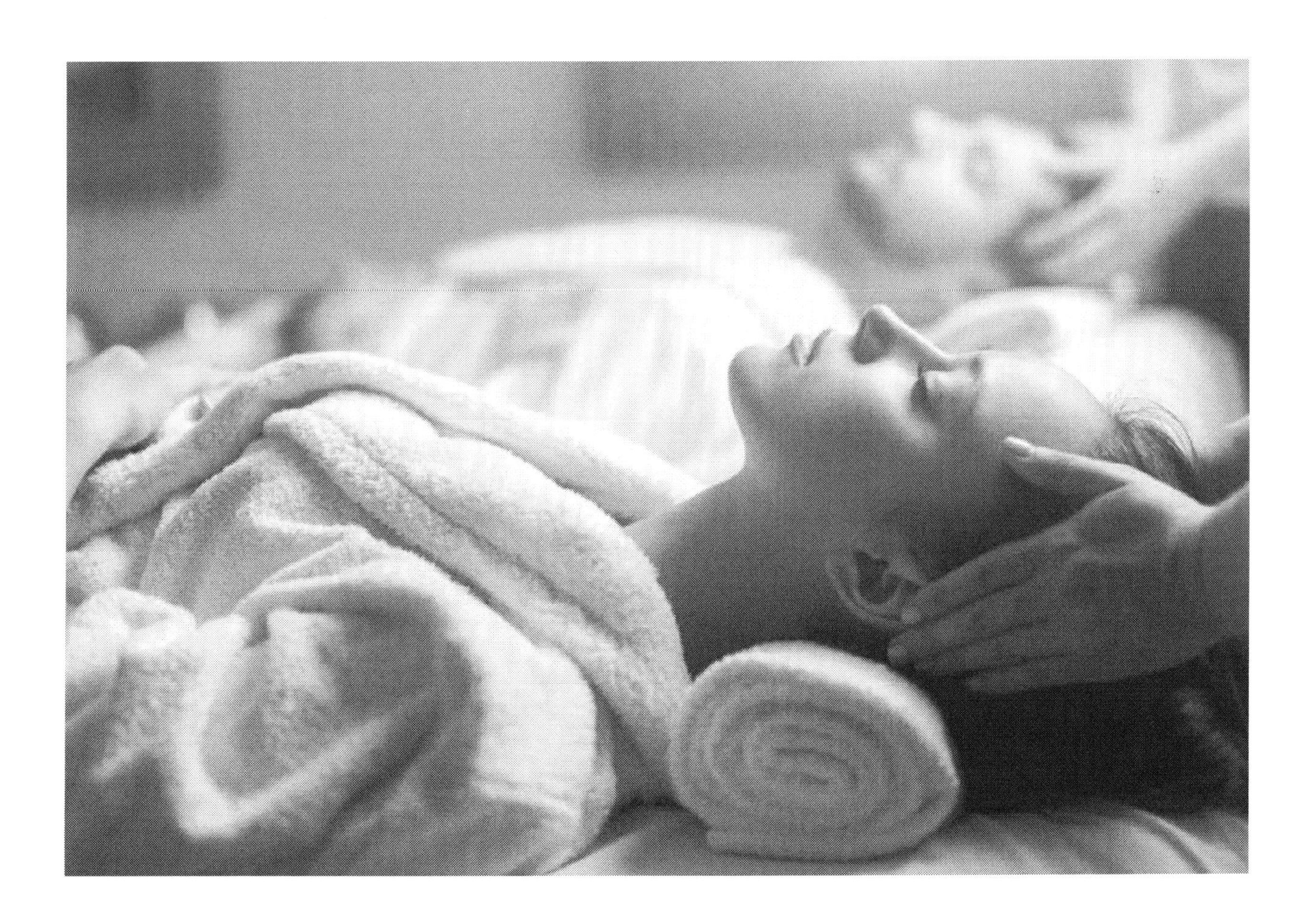

Dolphins, penguins, and sea lions swim across the azure seas of the Islas Ballestas. Invigorating treatments are available in wellness spas, gourmet seafood is served at fine dining establishments, and the sunsets are breathtaking.

Romantic Highlights: Explore Paracas town; day trip to Islas Ballestas; spa massages and therapies; fine dining at seafood restaurants; Paracas Natural Reserve; Huacachina.

2. **Cusco**

Cusco is brimming with the rich history and culture of Peru. It is one of the greatest spots for romantic getaways for seniors, and it is also a gateway to the stunning natural landscapes of Peru, all nestled under the Andes Mountains.

Colonial arcades abound in the lively main town plaza, enticing passers-by with vestiges of the pre-Columbian and Spanish eras. Magnificent churches predominate in Cusco, a city that is

deeply spiritual and religious. There are award-winning restaurants offering delicious Peruvian food and textile markets teeming with vibrant designs.
Cusco is a must-see destination because it combines a rich Peruvian past with the romanticism that visitors love.

Romantic Highlights: Explore the San Blas district; take a day trip to the Rainbow Mountain; visit the Qorikancha temple; do local craft shopping; and discover the Plaza de Armas.

3. **Sacred Valley**

A huge natural paradise, the Sacred Valley of the Incas stretches between Cusco and Machu Picchu.

Around the enormous valley and its typical hilltop settlements are the ruins of what was once the epicentre of the Incan Empire. Terraces of farms around verdant hills, and farmers continue to use time-honored farming methods. Peace will wash over you as you peruse the Incan Empire's artifacts; the valley exudes an air of peace.

Embark on a foot tour of the Sacred Valley and marvel at the breathtaking scenery, or saddle up and gallop through the villages, learning about their history and culture as you go.

Romantic Highlights: Day trip to Machu Picchu; Visit the Pisac ruins; Explore the Ollantaytambo ruins and village; Discover the Maras salt mines; Witness the Moray crop circles.

4. Puerto Maldonado

If honeymooning couples are planning to tour the Amazon Rainforest—the biggest tropical rainforest in the world—make sure to stop via Puerto Maldonado, Peru, their entry to the Amazon.

Before you go into the Dewy Rainforest, you should explore the city, which is rich in history and culture. Puerto Maldonado's easygoing vibe makes it a perfect destination for couples looking to spend some time together exploring the Amazon and its rich history. Immerse yourself in the vibrant nightlife, eat delicious local food, explore lively markets, and enjoy beautiful gardens.

But beyond Puerto Maldonado, you'll find plenty of chances to see animals and the rainforest, so they are the highlights. Join me on a journey into the Amazon as we see macaws at the clay lick, unusual wildlife at Lake Sandoval, and more.

Romantic Highlights: Day trip in the Amazon Rainforest; Visit the Macaw Clay Lick; Travel to Lake Sandoval; City walks and tours of museums

5. **Arequipa**

With its rich colonial past and stunning modern architecture, the city of Arequipa has long been touted as one of Peru's most romantic destinations, perfect for a honeymoon or romantic getaway.

The white-washed cityscape is composed mostly of sillar, a volcanic stone that was mined from the three Arequipa volcanoes. Museums tucked away in alleys reveal Arequipa's secrets, while Neoclassical cathedrals droop over bustling streets and Baroque architecture around the Plaza de Armas.

Arequipa serves as a portal to the breathtaking Colca Canyon, so couples may bask in the city's allure or explore the canyon's enormous mountains. As you take in the sights and sounds of Arequipa and its environs, the decision is entirely up to you.

Romantic Highlights: Discover the Plaza de Armas and historical center; Visit the San Camilo market; Enjoy views at the Yanahuara Scenic Overlook; Explore the Recoleta Convent; Day trip to Colca Canyon.

6. **Ica**

On their romantic Peruvian vacations, couples might find peace in the desert city of Ica, which is far off the usual route. In spite of the difficult desert climate, this ancient site has a booming agricultural business. Travelers are invited to explore the magnificent ambiance engulfing Ica at the museums and in the main town center. The amazing Huacachina desert village is located not far from the city.

Huacachina is unlike any other desert oasis that you will ever visit. On a romantic getaway, the little village nestled amid the changing dunes has something to boast about. One of the greatest things to do in Peru is to sandboard over the sand seas around the oasis, explore the verdant lagoon surrounded by palm trees, and traverse the desert to taste the finest wines from the renowned wine-making area around Ica.

Romantic Highlights: Tour the Oasis of Huacachina; Sandboarding in the Ica Desert; Wine-tasting in Peru's Best Wine Region; Stargazing; Dune Buggy across the Desert.

7. **Las Pocitas**

Las Pocitas, one of Peru's most breathtaking beaches, is located in the scenic Piura Region resort town of Máncora. Luxurious seaside hotels with lovely white beaches and deep blue oceans are perfect for couples seeking peace and quiet and the finest in coastal living.

Couples can take advantage of the beach's splendors throughout their stay on this section of the Peruvian coastline. Indulge in ceviche at picturesque beachfront restaurants, relax with soothing spa treatments, try exhilarating water sports or mild snorkeling, see whales jumping from the ocean at the correct time of year, and more.

Romantic Highlights: Kite surfing; tubing; fine dining; whale watching; spa therapies; snorkeling.

High gasoline prices on a road trip or rising hotel and airline fees due to increased demand are two examples of how travel may be costly.
Traveling doesn't have to break the bank if you follow these money-saving suggestions.

1. **Pack light**

Avoiding checked luggage costs is one clear benefit of traveling light, but there are many other reasons to do the same. As a first point, traveling light makes getting around much simpler. Carrying a small, lightweight bag makes you more nimble, so you can easily negotiate public transportation instead of worrying about how to pay for a cab.

So, what's the secret to taking little gear? Pack items that can be readily laundered in a sink. Choose garments that you can easily combine and that dry fast. So that you don't have to jam four pairs of shoes into your suitcase, stick to simple pieces that match with pretty much every outfit.

In addition, if you keep your luggage or bag as light as possible, you will be less likely to give in to the temptation to buy expensive trinkets.

2. **Shop at local grocery stores**

Experiencing a local market could be an exciting journey in and of itself. You may discover a wide variety of meals here that you would not find in your own kitchen. In addition, stocking up on food may help you save money. When you're not hungry, you're less inclined to purchase the pricey, stale muffin from the hotel café.

3. **Pack snacks**

The next best thing to going to the store is bringing snacks from home if you can't get to the store. To keep full on the go without taking up too much room in your suitcase, try protein-rich snacks like jerky and protein bars.

When you're on the go, bottled water may add up quickly as well. In the event that you are in an area with easy access to potable water, remember to bring your canteen and maybe even a collapsible water bottle.

4. **Get yourself into the airport lounge**

Dining in an airport lounge is a great way to satisfy your hunger while on the road. As an added advantage, users of the Priority Pass program are often eligible for lounge access with several premium travel credit cards. Light refreshments, including fruit, chips, cookies, and coffee, are often available; however, the quality varies at every lounge. On occasion, whole buffets are offered in the more upscale lounges.

Lounges provide more than just food; they also have Wi-Fi that is usually far faster than what the airport provides. Certain lounges also provide additional amenities like showers, gyms, and massage services. To make the most of the airport's facilities, arrive early.

5. **Arrive early**

Get to the airport well in advance of your scheduled departure time. Instead of utilizing public transit, which is usually cheaper, you could worry and hail an expensive taxi if you're running late. Depending on when you're going to the airport, you could discover that rideshare fares are higher. You may avoid the surge price if you give yourself extra time.

Stay on schedule to avoid the hassle of last-minute flight rebooking caused by tardiness.

6. **Get TSA PreCheck or Global Entry membership fees reimbursed**

To avoid the long lines at airports, sign up for TSA PreCheck or Global Entry. Both are versions of the U.S. Department of Homeland Security's Trusted Traveler program.

You may bypass the long security lines and go through security faster by using the accelerated lanes if you're authorized. These lanes don't require passengers to take off their shoes, computers, belts, or coats. Results from December 2021 show that almost all TSA PreCheck users (94%) had wait times of less than five minutes.

The application fees for TSA PreCheck and Global Entry are usually $85 and $100, respectively; however, TSA PreCheck's charge has been decreased to $78. You may get your money back with certain credit cards.

7. **Take advantage of credit card-free night certificates**

Free hotel stay vouchers are an enticement for several hotel credit cards, even ones with annual fees under $100. It could be a good idea to acquire one of these cards in order to save money and earn a free night's stay if the worth of your hotel room is more than the yearly cost (which it easily can be).

On top of that, these cards usually come with additional perks, such as elite status (which makes your stay even better) and bonus points (which may make future stays free or at least cheaper).

8. **Book hotel rooms on points**

Spending hotel points instead of saving them is usually the better choice when it comes to bonus points. Using points instead of cash to book a stay is a great way to save money on a holiday, but that's not all.

You may avoid resort fees: Inconveniently, some hotels charge guests more than $50 a night in resort fees for using extra amenities like pools and Wi-Fi. Fortunately, customers may use their points to book free stays via many hotel loyalty programs, such as World of Hyatt and Hilton Honors.

You might get extra discounts: Additional savings may become available for longer stays when using points to book your accommodations. For instance, when you stay at a Marriott hotel for five consecutive nights and pay using Marriott Bonvoy points, you get one free night of the lowest point value. Similarly, Hilton offers a promotion wherein customers with a Silver Elite membership or above get a fifth night free when using points to reserve a room.

9. **Travel during the offseason**

You can generally get cheaper deals and escape the crowds and hassles of peak-season travel if you plan your trip during the offseason. In the spring of 2021, NerdWallet analyzed more than 1,110 flights and discovered that, on average, Christmas travel was the costliest time to book.

On average, holiday-season airfare is 41% more expensive than non-holiday-season airfare when booked around six months in advance.

10. **Get a baseline understanding of typical costs**

Get a feel for the going rates so that an unofficial "tourist tax" won't surprise you.
One good example is to research typical cab fares online before you go to get a feel for the range. Before you go bargaining, it's a good idea to look into what other people usually pay for

similar products at the market. You may save money on bus fares if you know how to get legitimate tickets ahead of time.

11. Consider travel insurance

Travel insurance is a good investment if you're concerned about spending money you didn't have to pay for your trip. You have the opportunity to buy this insurance policy independently of your airfare.

Travel insurance is an added perk of using some credit cards to pay for things like airfare and hotel stays, so you may not even have to worry about paying for it out of pocket.

However, there are instances when not even travel insurance can provide a reimbursement. The only time you can get your money back is if you cancel due to an insured event, unless you shell out additional money for Cancel for Any Reason coverage.

CHAPTER NINE

BEST DAY TRIP FROM PERU IN 2024 (FROM A LOCAL!)

Indeed, Lima is a real adrenaline rush! We are certain that you could spend weeks exploring Lima due to the abundance of attractions and activities (we lived here for several months and never grew bored!).

However, it's a fact that many of Peru's top sites are really within easy day-trip distance from the capital! Yes, you should definitely get out of Miraflores and see more of Lima during your stay.

Actually, day excursions from Lima were some of our finest experiences in Peru. That is why we are so excited to tell you about them! Read this article to learn about the top day excursions from Lima that you should definitely do.

1. **Palomino Islands and swimming with Sea Lions**

When I'm in Lima, this is a must-do day excursion! This was unlike any other Lima trip I've been on before; I got to see amazing animals on the outside of the city, and I couldn't have been happier. The harbor in Callao is just 30 minutes away from Miraflores, so be prepared for traffic on your day excursion. From this point on, you may take a boat ride to the Palomino Islands.

Sea lions, penguins, and other marine birds call these islands home; they are situated about 15 kilometers (9 miles) off the coast of Callao. In fact, more than 10,000 sea lions call these islands home. When you get to the main island, you'll see hundreds of sea lions swimming and lounging about. Jumping into the sea is going to be the most thrilling aspect of this day excursion!

Sea lions are friendly, inquisitive, and lively creatures that will approach you to greet you. During our excursion, I saw sea lions who swam all around me and even bumped against me from under the water. Both thrilling and nerve-wracking, it was an experience like no other.

2. Huacachina and Ica Day Trip from Lima

Well, Huacachina, Peru, is really captivating. This picture of this small paradise—or "Oasis," as the locals name it—would be familiar to anybody who has read up on Peru. Located in the midst of rugged sand dunes, the little village of Huacachina is encircled by palm trees and a lake. It's mind-blowing and astonishing.

This itinerary really includes a day excursion to Huacachina and Ica, the bigger seaside city just adjacent to Huacachina, both of which are accessible from Lima. While the drive—about 3.5 hours each way—may seem daunting, you may take advantage of the air conditioning to unwind before seeing everything that these locations have to offer. Tours departing from Lima include a wide range of topics; however, my recommendation is to choose one that spends some time in Huacachina and maybe even stops at a winery in Ica (the birthplace of pisco!) for a sampling.

A dune buggy excursion and sandboarding are the top attractions in Huacachina. A specially designed buggy will whisk you over the sand dunes as you leap from one to another on this trip. The views are just stunning, and it's very thrilling! Sandboarding, which is similar to snowboarding but done on sand instead of snow, is an option you'll have at many stops along the way. Taking a stroll around the town's Oasis (lake) and stopping by one of the waterfront bars for a drink is also highly recommended.

For a full day of adventure, several trips include Huacachina and Ica, as well as the Ballestas Islands (more on this later). Not only is this trip reasonably priced, but it also comes highly recommended. This Lima-day travel itinerary covers all the must-see locations! Among Lima's full-day trips, this one is among the most thrilling.

If you're not up for the challenge of traveling to Huacachina, sandboarding on the dunes west of Lima is another option to consider. A full day of sandboarding is what you can expect on this excursion. Less time spent driving means more time on the board. However, the Ballestas Islands, the Oasis, and Ica will not be visible.

3. Ballestas Island (Poor Man's Galapagos) and Paracas Nature Reserve Tour

The Ballestas Islands are a great addition to a day trip to Huacachina if you're interested in nature. Paracas is a little village on the road from Lima to Huacachina, and these islands are just offshore from its shoreline. They host a wide variety of animals and are situated inside the Paracas Nature Reserve.

The Ballestas Islands have been dubbed "the poor man's Galapagos of Peru!" because of the abundance of species that inhabit these series of islands. The Blue-footed Booby is only one of numerous birds that may be seen here, much like in the Galapagos Islands. As an added bonus, you may see seals, sea lions, and penguins.

It takes three hours to travel from Lima to the Ballestas Islands, and then a short boat journey to get there. The whole island trip takes place aboard the boat and usually doesn't last more than thirty minutes.

This is why many Lima-to-Huacachina and Ica full-day tours include a boat tour of the Ballestas Islands. In addition to free time to explore the lake, this trip also includes a dune buggy ride from Huacachina. At just $139 USD per person, it's a fantastic full-day excursion from Lima that's also quite cheap.

4. Nazca Lines

You may take a day excursion from Lima to visit the Nazca Lines, which have long been on your bucket list! Although this Lima day trip involves a great deal of bus travel, it does allow you to view the Nazca Lines from above, which is a must-do for every traveler. This trip isn't for you if you're not familiar with the Nazca Lines; it's quite a journey. Just don't hesitate to book it if this is something you've always wanted to do in Peru!

Starting at 4 in the morning in Lima, this day tour gets going early! The early wake-up call shouldn't deter you, however. You'll be picked up in a cool van where you can relax and take it easy while your professional driver takes care of everything.
It will be time to board your picturesque plane to see the Nazca Lines once you get there. Taking a flight is definitely essential if you want to really enjoy this wonder.
On your return to Lima, you'll make a pit stop at Huacachina to go on a dune buggy trip, so the fun doesn't stop there either. In fact, this is a really unusual and full-day excursion from Lima. This Nazca Lines excursion may be booked in advance via their website; however, because of the limited party size restriction, early booking is highly recommended.

5. Pachacamac Ruins

You can reach Lima's Pachacamac Ruins by car in only half an hour from Miraflores. One of the top day excursions from Lima, this one delves into the fascinating history of the Incas, who once called this area home.
Having an expert walk us through historical locations is something I really like. Without one, I become a little lost and fail to appreciate the ruins for what they are.

This guided tour of the Pachacamac Ruins won't disappoint those who are interested in Peruvian history. Transportation to and from the ruins, including hotel pickup, is included in the approximately 4-hour tour.

If you are intending to visit Machu Picchu, this Pachacamac Ruins trip might serve as a wonderful introduction to Inca ruins.

TOP 10 MUST-VISIT MUSEUMS IN PERU

The rich cultural heritage and long history of Peru make it a fascinating place to visit. Peru is known for its breathtaking scenery and peaceful countryside, but the nation also has many great museums that can teach you more about its history, both ancient and modern, and the people who have lived here.

A number of Peru's most renowned museums are located in Lima, the country's cultural capital, but if you have the opportunity, you should also check out a handful in other regions. Because of this, we have made a list of the ten museums in Peru that we think are the most important for tourists to see.

1. **Museo de Arte de Lima (MALI), Lima**

Constructed between 1870 and 1871 for the express purpose of housing shows, the stunning Palace of the Exhibition houses MALI in Lima's central district. Starting with art from pre-Columbian times and continuing through around three thousand years of Peruvian history, the museum's permanent collection takes visitors on a journey through time. You must not miss this, one of Lima's most renowned museums.

2. **Museo de Arte Contemporáneo (MAC) , Lima**

For anybody interested in modern and contemporary art, a visit to Lima's MAC is a must. This museum, which opened to the public in 2013, showcases the work of Peruvian and worldwide artists working between the years 1950 and the present. Its mission is to facilitate dialogue between contemporary art and society. Architect Frederic Cooper created the structure, which is a masterpiece of modern architecture.

3. **Museo Larco, Lima**

There is an entire exhibit dedicated to ancient sexual ceramics in the Larco Museum in Pueblo Libre, which offers one of the most remarkable and interesting collections of Inca and pre-Inca antiquities. The museum boasts stunning grounds and a top-notch restaurant serving some of Peru's finest meals, in addition to its permanent collections of pottery, metals, and textiles.

4. **Museo Mario Testino (MATE), Lima**

MATE, located in Barranco, provides a modern take on traditional Peruvian art and cuisine. Founded in 2012 by its namesake, this museum is a non-profit organization with the dual goals of supporting Peru's creative future and preserving the country's significant cultural heritage. The museum often showcases the artwork of emerging Peruvian artists in addition to its permanent exhibitions showcasing Testino's renowned images.

5. **Museo Amano, Lima**

With a collection of textiles and artifacts that tomb raiders had dumped from Peru's numerous archeological sites, Mr. Yoshitaro Amano established this museum for the first time in 1964. One of the most remarkable collections of textiles and archeological artifacts from pre-Columbian periods is currently housed in the fully renovated room. Authentic Peruvian textile artifacts will be preserved, studied, and shared at the museum.

6. **Lugar de La Memoria, La Tolerancia and La Inclusión Social (LUM), Lima**

LUM in Miraflores, Lima, is a location that honors the internal war that took place from 1980 to 2000 for anyone interested in Peru's modern history. The museum highlights the significance of those 20 years in Peruvian history and shows how those events influenced modern Peru.

7. **Monasterio de Santa Catalina, Arequipa**

At the Monastery of Santa Catalina, one enters another dimension. The majority of the nuns who lived in the convent at its 1579 founding were Creole or mestizo. When the first Spanish nuns came, it was in 1964. Feeling totally apart from Arequipa, this outdoor museum has vibrantly colored buildings and meandering pathways that create the illusion of a little city.

8. Museo de Arte Pre-Colombiano (MAP), Cusco

This unique museum has over 450 fascinating artifacts ranging in period from 1250 B.C. to 1532 A.D., and it is housed in a colonial home that was constructed around an Inca ceremonial court. The objects on exhibit have been hand-picked from the Larco Museum's collection in Lima and are presented in eleven separate showrooms.

9. **Museo Inkariy, Sacred Valley**

Artists and archaeologists in Peru set out in 2002 to build the Inkariy Museum to showcase the country's remarkable pre-Columbian civilizations to the rest of the globe. The displays include contemporary language and easy-to-read materials, making this museum suitable for both adults and children. The museum also intends to display more than just the well-known Incas in order to highlight the variety of pre-Columbian civilizations. The Inca, Caral, Chavín, Paracas, Moche, Masca, Wari, Lambayeque, and Chimú civilizations are shown in this museum's several galleries.

10. Choco Museo, Cusco / Lima / Ollantaytambo / Pisac

Visiting the Choco Museum is an excellent choice for a family vacation. Visitors may enjoy free access to the choco museum's interactive cacao and chocolate exhibits, and if they want to learn more about the science and art of chocolate manufacturing, they can sign up for one of several seminars. Although Peruvian chocolate isn't very well-known, the country does export cacao. The Choco Museum teaches visitors about the whole chocolate-making process, from planting the cacao tree to tasting the finished product.

Peru has a rich and interesting history and is home to a wide variety of wildlife. One of the best ways to get a better understanding of Peru's rich cultural history is to stop by one of the numerous museums that dot the country.

CHAPTER TEN

7 DAYS IN PERU: AN ITINERARY FOR FIRST-TIME TRAVELERS

DAY 1: ARRIVAL IN CUSCO

After a brief flight from Lima, I arrived in the picturesque city of Cusco early in the morning and headed to Casa Andina, our accommodation for the night. Resting after the long journey from Zurich, I got up early the following morning to tour the city and meet up with the other travelers I would be spending the next week with. On the first day, we opted for a leisurely lunch at Jack's Cafe, a favorite spot for travelers and backpackers seeking a filling western-style meal with many vegetarian alternatives. We visited the Cristo Blanco monument in the evening, which overlooks Plaza de Armas, Cusco's main plaza, and the surrounding area. You may get some beautiful photos here with the 26-foot Jesus Christ statue, several llamas, and some ladies in typical Peruvian attire. The Church of San Cristobal is close by and provides similarly breathtaking views over the city, particularly when the lights are turned on at night. Nuna Raymi, a restaurant serving traditional Peruvian food that is within walking distance from our accommodation, served us supper.

DAY 2: SALINAS DE MARAS, CHINCHERO AND AGUAS CALIENTES

Allie M. Taylor's Perfect Seven-Day Peruvian Itinerary Allie M. Taylor's Perfect Seven-Day Peruvian Itinerary. We got an early start the next day so that we could see the dawn in Salinas de Maras, an old salt mine. Where residents still toil to collect and haul large sacks of salt up the hill to be processed and sold, I was astounded by the sight of hundreds of pastel-colored ponds dotted over the mountainside. After that, we stopped by the quaint village of Chinchero, where we saw local women weave exquisite textiles. Additionally, Chinchero has a fantastic artisan market where you can get a wide variety of colorful and lovely goods; I spent about 30 soles on a typical Peruvian sweater.

Lunch was a private affair at Mama Mary's restaurant and house in the heart of the Sacred Valley, where we spent the afternoon. After finishing our meals, we boarded a gorgeous train that would take us to Aguas Calientes in two hours. Along the way, we passed flowing rivers and saw mountains and forests. You can only reach the enchanted small village of Aguas Calientes by rail. This little town is the perfect place to stay if you're visiting Machu Picchu, so be sure to book your accommodation in advance if you want to avoid the crowds. Tierra Viva was a contemporary hotel with a great location, and we stayed there.

DAY 3: MACHU PICCHU

Surprisingly lower than Cusco, the Incan stronghold of Machu Picchu, which dates back to the 15th century, is located at 7,972 feet (2,430 meters). For what seems like an eternity, seeing Machu Picchu in person has been a goal of mine. We were hell-bent on going there first thing in the morning, but I underestimated how much preparation would be necessary. Observe these crucial points if you want to be at the site before dawn:

- You must wake up early (I set my alarm for 3:30 a.m.)

- If you want to catch the dawn bus, you need to be in line by 4:00 or 4:15 in the morning to guarantee a spot among the first 100 individuals. Taking one of the first four buses up the mountain is essential if you want to see the dawn at the peak in good time, as we discovered. I can't emphasize enough how crucial it is to come as early as possible; it was startling to see how many other people were already in line when we arrived at 4:15 a.m.

- While food is not officially permitted on Machu Picchu grounds, it is a good idea to pack warm clothing and breakfast to wear while you wait. As the sun rises, the temperature will climb, so dress in layers.

- Machu Picchu does not have any restrooms on site, so drink less water and go to the toilet before you go.

- Do not rush. You can't walk back up the one-way trail through Machu Picchu, so make the most of your time at the top viewpoint before descending to the ruins. It's a simple error that might completely derail the whole thing.

This natural marvel did not let us down with its breathtaking splendor, even if clouds prevented us from seeing the dawn we had hoped for. The enthralling and enigmatic past of Machu Picchu was also revealed to us. The construction of this structure is said to have begun in the mid-1400s, but it was left undiscovered until 1911, when the Spanish conquest began.

After seeing the ruins, we boarded a train to Ollantaytambo, a charming town known for its cobblestone alleys, ancient houses, and lively marketplaces. Before checking into the stunning Hotel Pakaritampu, we decided to take a stroll around town.

DAY 4: LLAMA BLESSING CEREMONY

We boarded the van the next morning and traveled for an hour to Latis Valley to take part in the traditional llama blessing ritual. The settlement we stopped at was the highest point we had reached so far on our journey, standing at an amazing 17,000 feet. The cultural richness and uniqueness of this encounter made it the standout of the whole trip, even though I wasn't sure what to anticipate.

Since this ritual occurs only twice a year during the birth of new llamas, few visitors have the chance to see it. The herd is the primary source of wool and food for the villagers; thus, this ritual is performed in the hopes that it will bring them good fortune and health. There was a lot of ceremonial dancing and singing, but the most moving part was when they wed two young llamas!

DAY 5: PISAC MARKET AND RUINS

We visited the picturesque village of Pisac the next day on our return to Cusco. Pisac is well-known for its textile market and its extensive Incan past. The market is a wonderful spot to get patterned sweaters and blankets created by locals in a rainbow of colors. Along with a turquoise ring, a scarf, and an additional sweater, I couldn't resist purchasing a few of the alpaca blankets to take home with me. A few of the females went as far as to purchase Moroccan-inspired carpets and throw pillows. We had a typical lunch in town and spent some time exploring the grounds of the nearby Incan ruins before returning to Cusco.

DAY 6: EXPLORING CUSCO

Our tour guide, Simon, gave us a fantastic walking tour of the city as we embarked on our last full day in Peru. We lost track of time, meandering through the city's cobblestone alleys and taking in every architectural detail. We were able to discover more about the Incan history and the Spanish Conquest on our tour of Cusco, which included stops at the Plaza de Armas, the Cusco Cathedral, and the Church La Compañía de Jesus. Do the same if you're in Cusco for an extended period; it's highly recommended.

Our journey came to a close at the San Pedro market, a one-stop shop for all things local, including chocolate, medicinal plants, handmade blankets and purses, and fruits straight from the region. On the way home, we stopped by the fruit booths to get some freshly squeezed orange juice, some delicious dried fruit and other treats.

We went to Rooftop Kitchen in the evening to learn how to make delicious local dishes like fish ceviche and quinoa risotto while watching the sun set over Cusco's rooftops. Because I think it's one of the greatest ways to explore the culture, I would suggest it to anybody looking for an unforgettable experience.

DAY 7: RAINBOW MOUNTAIN AND TRAVEL HOME

Images of Rainbow Mountain have been trending on Instagram for a while now, contributing to the mountain's meteoric rise to fame. In order to give us a more authentic experience away from the crowd, our tour guide decided to take us to a less frequented section of the "Rainbow.". To start our four-hour journey to the mountains, we got up quite early, at around 1 a.m. The trek to Rainbow Mountain was brief, but the views of Ausangate and the multicolored countryside below were breathtaking. Being able to witness the "rainbow-like" mountains in person for the first time without seeing a soul was an unbelievable experience. Before boarding the plane to return home, it was the ideal farewell excursion.

Made in United States
Troutdale, OR
12/11/2024